I WANT YOU

A COMMON SENSE GUIDE FOR PATRIOTS

by

James M. Watts

authorHOUSE

1663 Liberty Drive, Suite 200
Bloomington, Indiana 47403
(800) 839-8640
www.authorhouse.com

First published by AuthorHouse 08/04/04

ISBN: 1-4184-5663-2 (sc)

Library of Congress Control Number: 2004094296

Printed in the United States of America
Bloomington, Indiana

This book is printed on acid-free paper.

Table of Contents

INTRODUCTION

Our expanding role as the "world's keeper" is beginning to negatively impact both citizens and resources. Dynamic changes have been evolving since World War II and as our multi-task involvement expands the problems increase. Daily we read about the consolidation of businesses, factory closings, the loss of jobs or the lack of medical insurance. We are faced with insurmountable obstacles by countless countries and cultures that will never share our love for rule of law and the value of life, liberty and the pursuit of happiness.

It is important that we become aware of the inherent problems and as citizens help create and support possible solutions. Our direction is going to be very important over the next few years as our actions will determine the overall strength and stature of the United States for generations.

We have been operating under an "open door" policy since 1945 and the following chapters will address some of the most disturbing trends. My treatment of the subject can best be described as "focused isolationism". The agenda does not preclude continuing trade and relations with the world, it merely suggests that we address the many issues in a more nationalistic manner designed to place the interests of our citizens over those of other nations. Focused isolationism differs from the much-maligned policy of isolationism of pre World War II vintage, which basically promoted a "closed-door" society.

In addition to our foreign problems we have a number of important domestic issues demanding consideration. Both domestic and foreign issues are being addressed using a technique of research, defining the status of the U.S., comparisons with other nations and the presentation of recommendations for consideration and debate.

The following chapters are not directed specifically to members of political parties, gender, minorities, the young, the old, the affluent, the poor, the far right, the far left, the religious, specific races or creed. The statistics are being presented as they are with no regard to political correctness. The content, which is presented in plain language, will not be diluted or encumbered by social concerns, existing policies, the power of special interest groups, the media or world opinion. The book includes a number of statistics that reflect in a negative way upon the United States. These examples were used only to focus attention upon addressing current issues and potential problems. The United States remains the most powerful nation in the world from both an economic and military viewpoint. Hopefully, the book will help enhance and preserve our view from the top for time eternal.

The book is directed to those who have a desire to contribute in meaningful ways to the preservation of a strong and vibrant United States of America that fully reflects our values and protects our lifestyles. The scope of subjects included within the book is extensive. Volumes would be required to evaluate the tangled webs that have been created by millions of both well-intentioned and self-serving participants from around the world over the past fifty years. The intent of the book is to provide some basic data and projections for consideration as to potential problems within the future and to offer a few simplistic "common sense" solutions.

Likely some business executives, politicians, economists and academia will look upon this book with disfavor. It addresses many of the problems caused by the creeping emergence of a unified world society which has been endorsed by many.

The solutions are not being offered as "final solutions" but merely as catalysts or brainstorming concepts that will help to provide an atmosphere for the acknowledgment of problematic trends and the development of creative solutions with substance. Over time it is hoped that an aggressive mind set by substantial numbers of concerned citizens will help create new concepts, direction and energy for the rebirth of citizen involvement, innovative political platforms, honest political agendas and appropriate governmental action. A move towards focused isolationism could generate an agenda for both foreign and domestic issues that would maintain the prominence and well being of the United States throughout the millennium.

It is imperative that main street America becomes actively involved in the political process including ongoing communications with their elected officials. Time is of the essence as we must chart our future while we still maintain the strength and vitality of the world's greatest superpower.

Chapter One

Trade

Years ago I met Sam Walton, the founder of Wal-Mart, and his associate David Glass who later became the president of Wal-Mart. Mr. Walton and Mr. Glass were attending the National House Wares Exhibit which was one of their first buying conventions after switching from Ben Franklin Stores to their own Wal-Mart Stores. During those years the National House Wares Exhibit in Chicago was one of the largest trade shows in the World and attendance approached 80,000 people. The convention was held at McCormick Place and it provided a forum for viewing and purchasing a vast array of products. Domestic manufacturers and importers displayed their wares for primarily buyers representing multi-line distributors of products for distribution throughout the United States.

In the early years Wal-Mart supplied their manufacturing suppliers with "Made in USA" stickers for their products. Mr. Walton evidently had every intention that the manufacturers of the United States would be their predominate suppliers. Mr. Walton along with the rest of us had no idea of the overwhelming impact that Wal-Mart and other mass merchandisers would make upon the world economy. Years later in the world marketplace of 2004 the consumer driven market has reshaped the buying habits, economy and the landscape of many smaller towns within the United States.

During the early fifties GEM Stores located in Houston, Texas was one of the first mass merchandisers. GEM Stores were membership stores similar to Sam's or Costco Stores of today. Other regional retail operations across the United States changed their sales and marketing focus and moved into mass merchandising. K-Mart, a division of Kresge Stores, began operations during the same period as Wal-Mart and soon the mass merchandising concept of retailing was expanding rapidly offering virtually all of the volume products from the hard goods, soft goods and food industries.

To the average consumer the savings represented by volume purchases, efficient distribution and a large multi-product selection was and remains a win win situation. The age of consumerism has literally moved throughout the World and it will continue to expand geometrically.

The dynamic changes in retailing and distribution caused by the inception of mass merchants supported by consumer demand over the past forty years has been a significant factor in our balance of trade. Before mass merchandising the distribution flow of consumer goods was primarily from the manufacturer, to a regional distributor and finally to a local retailer. As many distributors and retailers were involved it was possible for a number of manufacturers to compete within the marketplace based upon style, packaging, pricing, location, performance and other considerations. The system supported numerous manufacturers, many distributors and a number of retailers on every town square.

Conversely, mass merchandising by its nature created an era of "consolidation". Over time, consolidation of distribution and sales by mass merchants replaced thousands of distributors and tens of thousands of retailers. That evolution still continues throughout the United States and it is increasing throughout the world. Consolidation of purchases forever changed the world marketplace and opened the doors to massive amounts of foreign imports. Following are the factors that led to increased purchases of foreign made products:

1. Large orders were placed with a limited number of manufacturers.
2. Orders were placed far in advance with extended shipping schedules.
3. Prices were intensely negotiated to obtain competitive price points.
4. Foreign governments increased intervention into commerce.
5. Low wages in foreign factories offered cost advantage.
6. The evolution of computers facilitated the consolidation process.

From a reality standpoint the above factors collectively have eliminated or are eliminating most of the U.S. domestic manufacturers of products. As a consequence our negative balance of trade continues to grow without restraint.

Other factors help fuel our trade deficit. The United States consumer's purchases of luxury automobiles, fine wines and state of the art electronics have proven that foreign makers have the ability to make and export very desirable products. The problem may be partially addressed by improvements in the quality of our domestic goods and increased efforts by our manufacturers as to consumer perception. However, the perceived status symbol of owning or consuming foreign products will always be a major factor for purchasing within the United States.

Consumers in many countries share a nationalistic desire to purchase products made within their country. Sadly, our consumers have proven that they have little allegiance and almost disdain for the more expensive products "made in the U.S.A". Unfortunately, our competitive lifestyle and the continuous media reinforcement of status symbols combine to make it virtually impossible to divert buyer preferences.

Another problem that confounds any major move to address our trade deficit problem are those within the United States that believe in the existing concept of "free trade". Evidently for some the system has served them well and they are not necessarily concerned about future generations.

In early 2004 a survey was done by the University of Maryland's Program on International Policy Attitudes. This survey (PIPA) is considered to be one of the most comprehensive U.S. polls on trade issues. The survey found that support for free trade fell from 1999 to 2004. The significant statistic came from those Americans making over $100,000 per year. This income group has traditionally been the most ardent supporters of free trade, however, the survey reported that support from this group declined from 57% to 28%. The poll also found that 33% of this group want free trade discontinued as compared to 17% back in 1999.

I just had a vigorous discussion with an acquaintance who truly believes that our problem is "that our wages are too high within the United States". I heartily disagree with that philosophy as I do not believe that any person that works within the United States should be in a position that would require them to adjust wages and lifestyles based upon wage scales in China or Cameroon.

Product development, research, automation and our high level of worker productivity offers some unique manufacturing and trade opportunities in selected industries. Industries such as the medical industry and our high tech computer oriented companies continue to be on the cutting edge of development and sales around the world. The expansion of our tech industries has been in place for a number of years. These industries offer our best as to creativity, the development of worthy products and our best opportunity to impact our negative balance of trade. The United States has had continuing losses within traditional industries and those losses collectively have been so massive that the positive impact of our high tech industries has been virtually lost in the numbers.

The following comparisons deal exclusively with exports, imports and the trade balance. They show the impact upon our balance of trade over the last fifteen years. I did not take into consideration the ownership of facilities both domestic and foreign as ownership is irrelevant within this presentation. My goal is to offer a vivid picture of the realignment of production facilities so that citizens of the United States will be in a position to understand more about the balance of trade problems that are more and more impacting their lives.

These statistics are from the International Trade Administration, which is a part of the U.S. Department of Commerce. The first chart shows the growth of our trade deficit. The trade deficit reflects the difference between the importing of goods into the United States and the exporting of goods from the United States to foreign destinations. In 2003 the United States exported $723,743,177,000 and imported $1,259,395,000,000 of goods. Our negative trade balance for 2003 was $535,652,466,000. These figures represent a deficit increase of 17% comparing 2002 as to 2003. Over the last ten years the negative balance has grown by four times and it has doubled during the last five years. My projections based upon future growth of the deficit are even more problematic.

The significance of the balance of trade deficit is that the figures are an indicator of our current and future marketability of products and goods around the world. An increase in the negative trade balance translates to fewer exports to the world market and continuing losses of industries, factories and jobs within the United States.

US/WORLD --- NEGATIVE BALANCE OF TRADE

YEAR		YEAR	
1989	- $109,631,021,000	1998	- $233,410,638,000
1990	- $103,061,785,000	1999	- $331,945,348,000
1991	- $67,019,679,000	2000	- $436,466,907,000
1992	- $84,546,403,000	2001	- $410,933,219,000
1993	- $115,610,544,000	2002	- $470,291,252,000
1994	- $151,414,528,000	2003	- $535,652,466,000
1995*	- $160,474,727,000	2008	- $1,000,000,000,000
1996*	- $168,487,634,000	2013	- $2,000,000,000,000
1997*	- $182,614,683,000	2018	-$3,000,000,000,000

* Estimates based upon historical increases.

PROBLEMATIC TRADING PARTNERS

China, Japan, the European Union (EU), the Organization of Petroleum Exporting Countries (OPEC), and our neighbors, Mexico and Canada represented 80.3% of our trade deficit during 2003. A percentage breakdown showing the 2003 balance of trade relationships follows:

PERCENTAGES OF 2003 NEGATIVE TRADE BALANCES

CHINA	EU	JAPAN	CANADA	OPEC	MEXICO	TOTAL
23.1%	17.6%	12.3%	10.2%	9.5%	7.6%	80.3%

CHINA

A friend of mine is the owner of an international company that supplies technical parts for the construction of heavy industry facilities. His company has five factories located around the world and they are a major global manufacturer of highly specialized parts that are required by numerous industries. He advised that 70% of their orders are destined for shipment to China. Based upon his in depth knowledge of projects on the drawing board and under construction he is convinced that China plans to dominate many industries. Their course of action is insured with readily available technical expertise from around the world, 1,200,000,000 people and ample natural resources. The following statistics clearly identify China as the most aggressive international competitor in the world.

It was reported in March of 2004 by Michelle Kessler of the *USA Today* that China has just recently initiated policies that will heavily impact the sale of U.S. made computer chips to China. A new law requires that all chips include a security technology licensed by Chinese companies. Secondly, they added a 17% value added tax to imported chips and thirdly, they are developing their own standards for cell phone networks and DVD players. Collectively these measures greatly inhibit the sale of U.S. made computer chips to China. This is only one example of a growing monopolist trend in China and we may expect similar measures in other industries.

8

US/CHINA --- TRADE BALANCE

YEAR	FROM CHINA	TO CHINA	BALANCE
1989	$11,988,535,000	$5,807,371,000	-$6,181,164,000
1990	$15,223,887,000	$4,807,332,000	-$10,416,555,000
1991	$18,975,798,000	$6,286,833,000	-$12,688,965,000
1992	$25,675,509,000	$7,469,573,000	-$18,205,936,000
1993	$31,534,834,000	$8,767,104,000	-$22,767,730,000
1994	$38,781,143,000	$9,286,759,000	-$29,494,383,000
1995	$45,555,432,000	$11,748,447,000	-$33,806,985,000
1996	$51,495,276,000	$11,977,921,000	-$39,517,356,000
1997	$62,551,934,000	$12,805,416,000	-$49,746,518,000
1998	$71,155,860,000	$14,257,953,000	-$56,897,908,000
1999	$81,785,930,000	$13,117,677,000	-$68,668,252,000
2000	$100,062,958,000	$16,253,029,000	-$83,809,929,000
2001	$102,280,484,000	$19,234,827,000	-$83,045,656,000
2002	$125,167,886,000	$22,052,679,000	- $103,115,207,000
2003	$152,379,239,000	$28,418,493,000	- $123,960,742,000
2008 *	$245,000,000,000	$40,000,000,000	- $205,000,000,000
2013 *	$345,000,000,000	$55,000,000,000	- $290,000,000,000
2018 *	$445,000,000,000	$70,000,000,000	- $375,000,000,000
2023 *	$545,000,000,000	$85,000,000,000	- $460,000,000,000

* Estimates based upon historical increases.

TOP FIVE EXPORTS SENT TO CHINA DURING 2003

Electric machinery etc. tv & sound equip.	$4,782,555,000
Nuclear reactors, boilers, machinery, etc.	$4,639,624,000
Oils seeds, misc. grains	$2,877,388,000
Aircraft, spacecraft and parts	$2,451,156,000
Optic, photo, medic instruments	$1,594,014,000

TOP FIVE IMPORTS RECEIVED FROM CHINA DURING 2003

Nuclear reactors, boilers, machinery, etc.	$29,902,035,000
Electric machinery etc. tv & sound equip.	$28,790,351,000
Toys, games & sports equipment	$16,104,542,000
Furniture, bedding	$11,824,429,000
Footwear	$10,565,175,000

A comparison of the exports vs. imports indicates that China predominately purchases industrial goods from the United States and ships us consumer goods. China represents a huge and rapidly growing marketplace for consumer goods and raw materials as demand will grow exponentially as does their household income. As China continues to expand their infrastructure massive amounts of products are going to be required. China will require products from the world marketplace and it is imperative that the United States use our full and considerable leverage as a key-trading partner to acquire an equitable and permanent trading relationship.

JAPAN

Japan has a reputation of unreasonably limiting imports, as they are very protective of their industries and agriculture community. In addition to their "closed" import policy their society traditionally will purchase Japanese products over foreign competition. To further compound the problem their long-term goals from their boardrooms exhibit a strong nationalistic protectionist philosophy as to the use of foreign parts or assemblies in their finished products. The following statistics indicate that the Japanese are past masters of maintaining a trade advantage with the United States. The figures vary as per year, however, our balance of trade is negatively impacted with a gain of approximately $1,500,000,000 each year.

US/JAPAN --- TRADE BALANCE

YEAR	FROM JAPAN	TO JAPAN	BALANCE
1989	$93,585,859,000	$44,583,917,000	- $49,001,942,000
1990	$90,433,130,000	$48,584,637,000	- $41,843,483,000
1991	$92,333,083,000	$48,146,512,000	- $44,186,571,000
1992	$97,181,357,000	$47,763,913,000	- $49,417,444,000
1993	$107,267,680,000	$47,949,465,000	- $59,318,216,000
1994	$119,149,366,000	$53,480,756,000	- $65,668,610,000
1995	$123,577,416,000	$64,297,852,000	- $59,279,566,000
1996	$115,218,106,000	$67,535,534,000	- $47,682,572,000
1997	$121,359,200,000	$65,672,594,000	- $55,686,606,000

1998	$121,981,583,000	$57,887,875,000	- $64,093,708,000
1999	$131,403,584,000	$57,483,535,000	- $73,920,049,000
2000	$146,576,678,000	$65,254,366,000	- $81,322,211,000
2001	$126,601,729,000	$57,639,072,000	- $68,962,657,000
2002	$121,494,231,000	$51,439,625,000	- $70,054,605,000
2003	$118,028,982,000	$52,063,765,000	- $65,965,217,000
2008 *	$125,000,000,000	$53,000,000,000	- $72,000,000,000
2013 *	$132,000,000,000	$55,000,000,000	- $77,000,000,000
2018 *	$138,000,000,000	$57,000,000,000	- $81,000,000,000
2023 *	$145,000,000,000	$59,000,000,000	- $86,000,000,000

* Estimates are based upon historical increases.

TOP FIVE EXPORTS SENT TO JAPAN DURING 2003

Nuclear reactors, boilers, machinery, etc.	$7,100,503,000
Electric machinery, sound & tv equipment	$5,962,511,000
Optic, photo, medical instruments	$5,454,565,000
Aircraft, spacecraft and parts	$4,845,534,000
Cereals	$2,384,604,000

TOP FIVE IMPORTS RECEIVED FROM JAPAN DURING 2003

Vehicles, except railway	$43,035,057,000
Nuclear reactors, boilers, machinery, etc.	$25,160,338,000
Electric machinery, sound & tv equipment	$19,323,691,000

Optic, photo, medical instruments	$5,935,410,000
Organic chemicals	$2,613,100,000

I was surprised that the top ten-export list to Japan includes a relatively small dollar amount of foodstuffs as the Japanese have limited land available and they do not practice modern agriculture techniques. The lead item on the top ten imports list is automobiles and this product amounted to sixty-five percent of our deficit problem with Japan during 2003.

The United States must gain reasonable access to the Japanese marketplace with our products or reduce Japanese imports to a reasonable level. Large trade deficits with Japan have been acceptable to the United States for many years and it will take a very determined effort to gain an equitable balance of trade with Japan.

EUROPEAN UNION

The fractured marketplace of Europe came together with the advancement of the common market within the last few years. Before 1996 the balance of trade with the European common market countries was not significantly out of balance. From 1989 through 1995 the United States actually had positive balances of trade for three years and deficits for four years. Since 1996 the increase in our negative balance of payments averages approximately

$10,000,000,000 per year. The troubling trend indicates imports are rising and exports are remaining constant:

US/EUROPEAN UNION TRADE BALANCE

YEAR	FROM EU	TO EU	BALANCE
1996	$142,718,448,000	$127,510,598,000	- $15,207,850,000
1997	$157,543,732,000	$140,803,150,000	- $16,740,581,000
1998	$176,366,609,000	$149,470,239,000	- $26,896,369,000
1999	$195,367,918,000	$151,644,903,000	- $43,723,015,000
2000	$220,366,419,000	$164,825,302,000	- $55,541,116,000
2001	$220,031,134,000	$159,174,885,000	- $60,856,249,000
2002	$226,115,451,000	$143,747,470,000	- 82,367,981,000
2003	$244,811,384,000	$150,549,349,000	- 94,262,035,000
2008 *	$275,000,000,000	$150,000,000,000	- $125,000,000,000
2013 *	$325,000,000,000	$150,000,000,000	- $175,000,000,000
2018 *	$375,000,000,000	$150,000,000,000	- $225,000,000,000
2023 *	$425,000,000,000	$150,000,000,000	- $275,000,000,000

* Estimates based upon historical increases.

TOP FIVE EXPORTS SENT TO THE EUROPEAN UNION DURING

2003

Nuclear reactors, boilers, machinery, etc.	$31,940,965,000
Electric machinery, sound & tv equipment	$16,161,714,000
Optic, photo and medical instruments	$15,474,594,000

14

| Aircraft, spacecraft, or parts | $12,481,498,000 |
| Vehicles, except railway | $9,410,873,000 |

TOP FIVE IMPORTS FROM EUROPEAN UNION DURING 2003

Vehicles, except railway	$36,823,519,000
Nuclear reactors, boilers, machinery, etc.	$36,734,272,000
Organic chemicals	$22,661,063,000
Pharmaceutical products	$20,549,560,000
Electric machinery, sound & tv equipment	$15,353,097,000

The importation of vehicles from Europe represents a problem as to our balance of trade with the European Union. The figures indicate that vehicles imported to the United States amount to 39% of the total trade deficit with the European Union.

OPEC (ORGANIZATION OF PETROLEUM EXPORTING COUNTRIES)

Before doing the research I envisioned that petroleum and OPEC would be a paramount problem and by far the major contributor to our balance of trade problems. However, statistically the oil imports are not as threatening as the trade problems with China, Japan and the European Union. The importation of petroleum can not be addressed by trade strategies. It is a function of consumption, supply and demand and in 2003 OPEC decided to reduce output and raise prices.

US/OPEC -- TRADE BALANCE

1994	- $12,695,552,000	1999	- $21,707,126,000
1995	-14,332,177,000	2000	-47,792,964,000
1996	-17,976,129,000	2001	-39,688,382,000
1997	-18,625,010,000	2002	-34,482,021,000
1998	-9,022,602,000	2003	-51,037,336,000

OUR NEIGHBORS - CANADA AND MEXICO

A few months ago I purchased a Buick automobile and I thought naively that I was buying a good Detroit made automobile. A month or so later I discovered that the engine was made in Mexico and the automobile was assembled in Canada. NAFTA was signed in 1993 and it was designed to open the borders for more trade between the United States, Canada and Mexico. It required a couple of years before our domestic based industries could shift manufacturing to Canada and Mexico. By 1995 substantial factory relocations had been made as the trade deficit with our neighbors increased dramatically. NAFTA it appears did promote trade but unfortunately most of the trade flowed into the United States.

US/CANADA/MEXICO --- TRADE BALANCE

YEAR	CANADA	MEXICO	BALANCE
1995	-$19,094,573,000	- $15,393,543,000	- $34,488,116,000
1996	-$23,921,917,000	- $16,202,367,000	- $40,124,284,000
1997	-$17,926,132,000	- $14,494,034,000	- $32,420,166,000
1998	-$20,691,601,000	- $15,698,579,000	- $36,390,180,000
1999	-$34,411,209,000	- $22,662,448,000	- $57,071,657,000
2000	-$52,779,487,000	- $24,189,656,000	- $76,969,143,000
2001	-$53,244,353,000	- $29,923,882,000	- $83,168,235,000
2002	-$49,790,418,000	- $37,201,572,000	- $86,991,990,000
2003	-$54,685,133,000	- $40,615,877,000	- $95,301,010,000
2008 *	-$68,000,000,000	- $52,000,000,000	- $120,000,000,000
2013 *	-$85,000,000,000	- $67,000,000,000	- $152,000,000,000
2018 *	- $102,000,000,000	- $82,000,000,000	- $184,000,000,000
2023 *	- $120,000,000,000	- $97,000,000,000	- $219,000,000,000

* Estimates based upon historical increases.

TOP FIVE EXPORTS SENT TO MEXICO & CANADA DURING 2003

Vehicles, except railway	$45,660,643,000
Nuclear reactors, boilers, machinery, etc.	$47,562,991,000
Electric machinery, sound & tv equipment	$38,128,206,000
Plastics	$14,750,557,000
Optic, photo, medical instruments, etc.	$9,384,199,000

TOP FIVE IMPORTS FROM MEXICO/CANADA DURING 2003

Vehicles, except railway	$78,217,806,000
Mineral fuel, oil	$56,893,909,000
Nuclear reactors, boilers, machinery, etc.	$33,377,263,000
Electric machinery, sound & tv equipment	$32,887,700,000
Wood	$10,384,690,000

An analysis of trade categories indicates there are two products that collectively were responsible for our trade deficit with Mexico and Canada. Mineral fuel can not really be addressed, however, vehicles shipped to the United States amount to 82% of the Canadian/ Mexican deficit.

SUMMARY

The purpose of these statistics, that were available on the U.S. Commerce Department web site, is to illustrate that trade balances are a reflection of our ability as a nation to sell products throughout the world. If we continue to lose our share of the world market we will continue to lose industries, factories and jobs within the United States.

During January of 2004 The European Union, Japan, Canada and others ask the World Trade Organization to authorize punitive duties on the United States. This penalty is for industry reimbursements paid by our government directly to affected U.S. manufactures under the Byrd amendment, which was passed by Congress in 2000.

The World Trade Organizations has threatened to impose penalties upon the United States of $4,000,000,000 unless we repeal the amendment. I found it troubling that three of our trading partners with huge balances of trade in their favor should be the leaders of protest with the World Trade Organization on the Byrd amendment issue.

The balance of trade statistics over a fifteen year period clearly indicate that any and all actions by our government concerning trade, trade negotiations, trade treaties, and our involvement with the World Trade Organization have been a complete disaster. Clearly, any trade relief that the United States obtains is not going to be through the World Trade Organization. The United States is going to be required to make definitive decisions and dictate, not negotiate the new rules of trade engagement.

SOLUTIONS

I began to develop separate recommendations for each of the key trading partners based upon the size of our deficit, the rate of growth of the deficit and the products involved. It occurred to me that is exactly what we have been doing unsuccessfully over the years. Our strengths and weaknesses at the bargaining table has been exploited by trading partners and a litany of social and other considerations have convoluted equitable trade agreements. Whatever we do with trade reform it must firmly apply equally to all nations and to all products with the exception of petroleum:

OPTION ONE

Option One is based upon the premise that what is fair for one trading partner is fair for all. It is designed to reward those nations who trade equitably with the United States and penalize those nations who do not. The option addresses the ongoing problem of trade deficits with low wage nations, it provides the leverage to open and expand previously closed or restricted markets and it controls the future growth of deficits between the U.S. and our trading partners.

Let us suppose that the United States proclaims to the world with ample advance warning that beginning on January 1, of any given year that we will allow imports from each country of origin based upon their exports from the United States during the previous year. An analysis of the statistics suggests that the United States allow imports at a ratio of one and one-half times our exports to the subject nation for the previous year.

An example follows:

Nation X purchases U.S. exports totaling $500,000,000 of goods in year 2004. During 2005 the United States will allow imports from Nation X of goods totaling $750,000,000.

OPTION TWO

Impose a value-added tax upon all imports except petroleum. The consumers of the United States would pay the value added tax.

OPTION THREE

Impose import duties on all foreign goods except petroleum. Foreign manufacturers would pay these duties directly to the U.S. government.

OPTION FOUR

Impose store tax on all imported goods except petroleum. U.S. retail stores and auto dealers would pay this tax.

OPTION FIVE

Allow federal tax exemptions for new or upgraded manufacturing facilities within the United States. The U.S. taxpayer would subsidize the cost of these exemptions.

The global trading community and the World Trade Organization will protest vigorously upon the mention of any of the above options. The statistics show precisely what the world trading community has managed to arrange for their benefit over the last fifteen years. The United States has the right and obligation to our citizens to adjust our trade policies for our best interests and to determine our own destiny.

The lifeblood of any nation is the continuing spin of the wheels of commerce. The United States can not survive over the ages as a wholly transformed service nation regardless of what we are being told by the politicians and barons of the world economy. Consider the statistics, the inherent problems, the future of the United States and join the ranks of those who want to promote equitable trade for the United States on a worldwide basis.

Chapter Two

Jobs

The International Labour Office in Geneva, Switzerland, which is the labor agency for the United Nations, issued a press release early in 2004 that unemployment within the world was higher in 2003 than any period since the inception of reporting in 1990. They reported that 185.9 million or 6.2% of the total worldwide labor force was unemployed and also an estimated 550 million workers earned less than one-dollar per day.

It is evident that jobs are going to be more difficult to obtain and even though the United States is expected to begin an economic resurgence in early 2004, all of the experts warn of a continuing shortage of jobs. Concern should be shown for both unemployment and the quality of jobs available within the United States. Service jobs pay less than industrial jobs and as the proponents of world economy move us forward as a service oriented nation it is unlikely that our displaced industrial workers will be able to maintain their median household income. Offshore outsourcing has also entered into the equation as it directly effects the white-collar workers within the information technology industry.

The lack of jobs affects society in a number of ways and unemployment among youth is the most volatile scenario. According to the International Labour Office youth tend to be unemployed at a ratio of two to two and one-half times their national unemployment average. In 2003 there were estimated to be 88.2 million youth between the ages of fifteen and twenty-four unemployed. This is partiality troublesome when you consider that this is the age group that is the most subject to radical political persuasions and acts of violence.

The United States has been successful over the years with the exception of the depression era in being able to provide a relatively high level of employment at decent wages. The United States needs to be especially vigilant over the next few years as job opportunities are going to vary according to our successes in correcting the trade deficit, controlling offshore outsourcing, and improving our general economic conditions.

There are two major indicators concerning job opportunities and the quality of the jobs within the United States. The first is unemployment statistics and by percentages they reflect how many workers were unemployed during the year. The following chart includes unemployment statistics for the United States and other key nations:

UNEMPLOYMENT STATISTICS

	1998	1999	2000	2001	2002	2003
CANADA	8.3%	7.6%	6.8%	7.2%	7.7%	7.4%
CHINA	---------------- n/a ----------------				4.0	3.3
EUROPEAN UNION	9.9	9.1	7.8	7.4	7.6	8.8
JAPAN	4.1	4.7	4.7	5.0	5.4	5.4
MEXICO	3.5	3.2	2.2	2.7	1.9	3.3
FRANCE	11.8	11.2	9.3	8.5	8.7	9.4
GERMANY	9.3	8.6	7.8	7.8	8.2	10.0
ITALY	11.8	11.4	10.4	9.4	9.0	8.5
UNITED KINGDOM	6.3	6.1	5.4	5.0	5.1	4.9
UNITED STATES	4.5	4.2	4.0	4.7	5.8	5.9

Statistics are from: OECD, Latin Focus, U.S. Dept. of Labor, Labour Force Survey and United Nations Statistics Division.

To further substantiate our rising unemployment figure following is a chart showing the steady increase in unemployment benefits paid over the past few years:

STATE UNEMPLOYMENT INSURANCE BENEFITS

1990	1995	2000	2001	2002
$18.1 billion	21.2	20.5	31.6	42.0

Statistics are from: U.S. Census Bureau

To summarize the statistics; The United States unemployment rate has slowly been rising while most of the European Union unemployment figures with the exception of Germany have been dropping. The Chinese government recently advised that there past statistics were faulted and included are the most accurate figures available. Canadian and Mexican unemployment has been dropping since NAFTA. China and Japan both enjoy considerably lower unemployment figures than the United States and the numbers reinforce their trading agendas. Both nations are maintaining high levels of employment by successfully controlling their balance of trade.

MEDIAN HOUSEHOLD INCOME

The second major indicator of the health of the labor market is household income. The quality of jobs is reflected by household income statistics, which track the income of household members over fifteen years old. The income figures include wages, salaries, self-employment income, interest, dividends, income from royalties, trust income, social security and pensions. Median Household Income is expressed as an average dollar amount taken from all of the household incomes within the United States during a specific year.

Following is a chart showing the median household income of the United States. For comparative purposes a few other nations have been added:

MEDIAN HOUSEHOLD INCOME

	1985	1995	2000	2001	2002
UNITED STATES	$23,618	$34,076	$42,148	$42,900	$42,409
SWITZERLAND			64,400		
JAPAN			61,120		
FRANCE		60,610			
SOUTH KOREA			47,769 (1998)		
CANADA			43,413 (1999)		
GERMANY			42,702 (1998)		
UNITED KINGDOM			27,750 (1999)		

The United States has enjoyed a constant growth of median household income over the years. It is important that for the first time during the time frame of this report the United States has experienced a median household income less than the prior year. During 2002 the reported amount of $42,409 was less than the 2001 figure of $42,900. Later in 2004 the 2003 figures will be available and it will be interesting to see if a trend emerges. As our proponents of a World economy strive to convert the United States from an industrialized nation to a service nation we may expect further reductions in the median household income.

It is a fact that service industry jobs do not pay as well as goods-producing workers and this is confirmed by reports issued by the U.S. Department of Labor. An example of our transfer of jobs from industrial to service industries is contained within an article written by Sherri Day of the *New York Times* on December 10, 2003. It said "since the beginning of August, the restaurant business ... has accounted for eighteen percent of the 300,000 jobs created in the nation." Unfortunately, restaurant jobs are traditionally low paying positions and most of those employed will join the ranks of the low income.

LOW INCOME

All of the combined problems of a trade deficit, losing jobs to foreign countries and moving to a service nation affect many people. Most of all it impacts blue-collar workers who become unemployed as part of the loss of an industry within the United States. If a textile mill or a steel mill closes; it is virtually impossible for those workers to find gainful employment that will compensate at an equivalent pay scale. The loss of jobs breeds poverty, crime and adds to the roll of low-income families.

Poverty is a growing problem within the United States and for the second consecutive year the poverty rate rose from 11.7% in 2001 to 12.1% in 2002. The number of poor increased by 1.7 million to 34.6 million in 2001.

The United Nations has a published goal, which is to halve the number of people living in poverty by 2015. This is a commendable social objective; however, the redistribution of wages must not be at the further expense of the already too generous citizens of the United

States. We have a growing poverty problem within the United States and it will continue to grow exponentially as does our conversion to a service oriented society. As a nation our goal must be to address the needs of our fellow citizens, to vigorously protect our industries and jobs and to improve the betterment of our society.

LOSING FACTORIES OFFSHORE

Katherine Boo writing in *The New Yorker* early in 2004 did an article of the closing of a textile mill in Texas and the trials and tribulations of the workers seeking employment. Fruit of the Loom, a hundred-and fifty-three year old company, currently owned by Warren Buffett's Berkshire Hathaway closed the factory employing eight hundred workers. The factory had produced Levi's; Wrangler jeans; Carter baby clothes; Converse sneakers; Dickies uniforms, Vanity Fair lingerie; North Face parkas and Haggar slacks. Most of the production is being moved to Honduras and obviously the main factor in the move was the cost of labor. Economically this strategy will likely produce results in the boardroom but it is an economic disaster for eight hundred families.

NORTH AMERICAN FREE TRADE AGREEMENT (NAFTA)

Nafta went into effect in 1994 and since then our trade deficits with Mexico and Canada have increased as addressed in chapter one. As a specific example the textile industry in the United States has lost in the last seven years 190 textile factories located primarily in North Carolina and South Carolina. Employment within the industry has dropped from just over 500,000 jobs in 1990 to about 236,000 for a loss of approximately 250,000 workers since the inception of Nafta. Mexico exported to the United States in 1990 about $700,000,000 in textile products and since Nafta that figure has risen in 2003 to $7,200,000,000. The above statistics were provided by the American Textile Manufacturing Institute, the Department of Commerce and the Bureau of Labor Statistics.

WORKERS FROM MEXICO

Early in 2004 President Bush suggested a program allowing workers from Mexico the opportunity of working in the United States on a temporary basis. A program is long overdue, as the enforcement of border security is impossible and according to a 2003 report from the Immigration and Naturalization Service they estimate that seven million illegal immigrants are now in the United States. Of the total they estimate that 70% are from Mexico and that illegal entry increases by approximately 300,000 annually. Our border agents have the ability to apprehend the illegal aliens, however, without serious penalties for illegal entry enforcement becomes ineffectual.

The problem of illegal workers is compounded by the lack of cooperation from U. S. business owners who hire illegal workers, usually as contract workers, at low wages and no benefits. Legislation was passed in 1986 that provided civil and criminal penalties for those hiring illegal workers; however, it is evident that the penalties were not severe enough. Due to their non-legal status the illegal workers have none of the protection afforded our workers nor do they pay for the social services that they have available in some states. The Mexican workers have proven over the years that they are hard working and responsible. They fill a labor demand within the United States and it is in the best interests of the United States to develop a mutually beneficial plan.

Canada has a Foreign Worker program, as every year they require substantial numbers of foreign workers to supplement their work force. Their plan requires that foreign workers must have a job offer from a Canadian employer plus a work permit issued by Citizenship and Immigration Canada. Foreign workers are covered by the same federal and provincial labor standards as Canadian citizens. Foreign workers are also required to pay Canadian taxes. Under the skilled worker provision of the Canadian program an employer may offer a permanent job to a foreign employee. Working under this preferred status can lead to a permanent Canadian residency status. The Canadian program is a workable program that has been time tested. It should be considered as a model for our entry into the legal employment of foreign nationals.

The United States has always been the haven for those who seek a better life and we have literally opened the doors to the world. Unfortunately, as jobs become more scarce it will be necessary to control the flow of foreign workers and to collect revenue from them.

Foreign workers use our resources during their presence within the United States and it is only right that they pay a fair share.

A plan like the Canadian plan would be a great point of beginning. Due to the clouded history with U.S. employers and their general lack of compliance with the 1986 legislation it is going to be absolutely necessary to demand and enforce the complete cooperation of foreign worker employers. Employers must be required to follow the requirements of a United States Visiting Worker Program or be subject to severe monetary penalties and or face the possibility of being barred from future foreign worker employer activities.

H1-B VISA WORKERS

I would wager that only one American out of 10,000 has ever heard of this special visa that allows foreign nationals to legally work in the United States. I certainly had never heard of the program and during my research I found on the internet a panel discussion that was held in 2003 by Lou Dobbs of *CNN*. The visa program began back in the early 1990s and the justification was that there were not enough American workers to adequately staff all of the high tech industries. Our government created the H1- B visas which allowed college educated foreign workers to enter and work within the high tech industry. Initially we allowed 65,000 workers annually and later up to 190,000 annually under the program. Some still reinstate their annual visas, however, many remain illegally. It is estimated that currently there are one million illegal workers in the United States that entered and remained due to the H1-B program.

The H1-B visa program and the presence of the illegal workers is unacceptable and a solution is that our Department of Immigration make every effort to locate and deport the illegal workers. A good point of beginning would be a required reporting system from employers within the high tech industries. Substantial monetary penalties for company noncompliance is necessary as it is reported that the H1-B workers were preferred by employers because of the workers desire to remain within the United States.

OFFSHORE OUTSOURCING

Early in 2004 Treasury Secretary Snow made the comment that out-sourcing was an integral part of a global trading system. He went on to say "It's one aspect of trade and there can't be any doubt about the fact that trade makes America strong". I would highly recommend Secretary Snow read my first chapter on Trade. I can not by any stretch of the imagination see how foreign trade as currently manifested within our society does anything but draw down on our industries, factories, jobs and per capita income. With substantial loses in personal income taxes are going to be negatively impacted and the United States is going to be the largest debtor nation in the world with a decreasing tax base.

In April of 2004, *USA TODAY* reported that IBM had announced plans to acquire Daksh eServices of India. The deal which is scheduled to close in May would expand the IBM staff in India to about 15,000 providing that all of the 6,000 workers of Daksh are hired by IBM. This follows an early January 2004 article in The *Wall Street Journal* reported that IBM has discussed saving millions of dollars by moving thousands of U.S. Jobs offshore. The article was written after internal documents were obtained by the *Wall Street Journal*. The documents show that IBM executives expected to save $168 million per year starting in 2006.

The IBM report is just one of the daily commentaries we are beginning to read or view on the use of offshore outsourcing by major U.S. companies. *CNMONEY* reported in early 2004 that the consulting firm Forrester Research predicted that, in the next fifteen years, 3,300,000 U.S. service industry jobs and $136,000,000,000 in wages will move offshore to low wage countries such as India, China and Russia.

Computerworld reported in 2003 that an assessment by Gartner Inc. at an outsourcing conference confirms that 80% of U.S. companies will have high-level discussions about outsourcing in 2004. They also confirmed that within the near future 40% of those would have offshore outsourcing programs at various levels of implementation.

In April of 2004 it was reported by TEC International that a survey conducted by them of 1,091 CEOs received the following responses. The question was asked what jobs do you plan to outsource in the next twelve months? The response was manufacturing 12%, information technology 5% and customer's support/sales 4%.

In an article written by Matt Krantz of *USA Today* he quoted Ashish Thadhani, an analyst at Brean Murray Research. Mr. Thadhani said that there are three pioneers of off shoring: American Express, Citigroup and General Electric. He estimates that GE saves $340 million a year by utilizing 20,000 employees in India.

Apparently our government is taking a neutral position on offshore outsourcing as we are not seeing opposition from our government. *Computer Weekly.com* reported that Chris Israel, a deputy assistant secretary to the U.S. Department of Commerce commented during an ITAA (Information Technology Association of America) panel meeting the "the answer to economic challenges is growth and innovation". He made this statement even though he stated further that he understood the ramifications of offshore outsourcing such as salary reductions within the United States and a reverse brain drain on U.S. talent.

One of the foremost arguments made by outsourcing proponents is that within the United States we do not have adequately trained personnel to staff all of the IT positions required. In that same meeting of September 2003, Mr. Phil Friedman, chief executive officer of Computer Generated Solutions made this comment. His firm recently advertised to fill three hundred information technology positions and they received three thousand applications within three days. His further comment was that "One morning we will wake up ten years from now and we will not have the skills needed to support the infrastructure of this country". Priscilla Tate representing Information Technology executives, argued that offshore development is taking a toll on U.S. workers.

On January 7, 2004, Carly Fiorina, chief executive for Hewlett-Packard Co. spoke at a Washington D.C. forum for leading technology officials. Her comment was "There is no job that is America's God-given right anymore, we have to compete for jobs". At the same meeting as reported by Ted Bridis of the Associated Press, Craig Barrett, chief executive of Intel, stated that the United States "now has to compete for every job going forward". The overall intent of the meeting was to urge Congress and the Bush administration not to impose new trade restrictions on offshore outsourcing.

A general comment made by the group was that imposing trade barriers "could lead to retaliation from trading partners and even an all-out trade war". A spokesperson for a group representing Intel Corp., IBM, Dell Inc. and Hewlett-Packard made the comment "Countries that resort to protectionism end up hampering innovation and crippling their industries, which leads to lower economic growth and ultimately higher unemployment." The self-serving interests of this select group is understandably evident. Unfortunately, for the average American the trade statistics in chapter one confirm that we have been in a trade war for many years and we have lost virtually all of the battles. The United States is right now facing lower economic growth and experiencing higher unemployment and our

36

government has the audacity to tell us that growth and innovation is the answer. I doubt that creditors of an unemployed worker will accept for payment a comment that we are going to have growth and innovation.

The opposition at the meeting, Marcus Courtney, the president of the Washington Alliance of Technology Workers made this comment "This is not a recipe for job creation in this country, this is a recipe for corporate greed".

According to the planners of the new World economy the United States was supposed to have been the service nation of the world after our reduced role as an industrial power. Unfortunately, the lure of low wages and increased profits is evidently so irresistible to corporate profit centers that the problems of offshore outsourcing are growing daily.

Opposition to offshore outsourcing is growing as recently the State of Indiana rescinded a contract with an Indian firm and other states are considering legislation to prevent the use of taxpayer dollars for foreign contracts. Public opinion and legislation usually follow overt actions by others as social and economic problems appear as a result of those actions.

Early in 2004 another form of outsourcing came into focus. The city of Salt Lake City, Utah recently completed construction of a new 87,000 square foot library costing $65,000,000. The library is built from concrete panels that were formed in Mexico and shipped via truck to Salt Lake City. The Mexican manufacturer of the concrete panels is currently bidding on a hospital in Dearborn, Michigan and a federal courthouse in Springfield, Massachusetts.

The issue of offshore outsourcing is an increasingly serious problem and following are some measures that could be taken:

OPTION ONE

I do not believe it is possible to control offshore outsourcing by trying to establish barriers through the outsourcing companies or foreign countries. There are too many ingenious paths within the IT industry that the control of data transmission is virtually impossible. To place taxes upon the outsourcing companies would lead to tax manipulations or the establishment of offshore offices. The only place where control is possible are the U.S. firms that contract for offshore outsourcing. As an example, let us suppose that ABC Accounting wanted to use outsourcing. I recommend the following:

Legislation would require that ABC would be subject to a federal user tax amounting to 100% of the total value of their offshore outsourcing contract. The user tax would be similar to a sales tax and it would be due and payable upon signing the contract. It is interesting that India, which is one of the most aggressive suppliers of offshore outsourcing, has a 100% tariff on all imports. It seems appropriate that we reciprocate with a like amount.

OPTION TWO

A possible solution could be based upon the formula as presented in chapter one that would allow imports to the United States in proportion to purchases by a trading partner the previous year. As an example, if China purchased $100,000,000 of goods from the United States in 2005 then they would be entitled to export to the United States $150,000,000 of goods in 2006. The plan was developed for manufactured products, however, the program could be amended to include offshore outsourcing. Controls would again be required through the U.S. purchasers of offshore outsourcing and substantial penalties must be in place to insure that all transactions are reported.

TRADE UNIONS

Trade Unions contributed to the prosperity of the United States as they provided a service to workers and industries during the period of our industrial expansion. In a recent discussion it was pointed out to me that the prices of our products were to high because of union worker wages. Prices did rise as a result of union wages, however, a working relationship developed between unions and management. Together they developed the most productive and wealthy nation in the world.

Unions have remained a major factor within the European community and excessive vacation time and holidays have directly affected there productivity. Union membership statistics for the

United States follows and since the high point of membership in 1945 the percentage of total labor force has continually dropped:

UNITED STATES TRADE UNION MEMBERSHIPS

YEAR	MEMBER NUMBERS	% OF LABOR FORCE
1935	3,584,0001	3.2%
1945	14,332,000	35.5
1955	16,802,000	33.2
1965	17,299,000	28.4
1975	19,335,000	23.8
1985	16,996,000	18.0
1995	16,360,000	14.9
2000	16,258,000	13.5
2002	16,107,000	13.2

Statistics are from U.S. Bureau of Labor Statistics

SUMMARY

For several years the world economy proponents have been poised for the redistribution of industrial power throughout the world and it is happening. As our industries disappear the United States has been traditionally considered the emerging service oriented nation of the world. With the explosive growth and popularity of offshore outsourcing it would seem that our perceived role as the leading service nation is being vigorously challenged primarily by low wage nations. These dynamic changes affecting both our blue-collar and white-collar jobs cause deep concern and cast doubt as to what is going to be the future role remaining for the United States?

A job is one event that can offer hope and foster dreams for an individual. Conversely, the lack of a job leads to despair, lack of self worth, disregard of responsibilities and crime. The United States has been able to offer more work opportunities than any other nation and jobs have been the lifeblood of our nation. With all of the challenges of the world market it is time to make serious decisions as to the future of jobs within the United States. The standard of living of the United States and the very lifeblood of our industries and communities will be seriously impacted if American workers are forced to compete on the world market. It is impossible for workers to sustain a reasonable living wage when competing with Honduras or Mexico. To maintain a job base that includes living wages it is going to be necessary to take decisive action to eliminate corporate incentives for moving U.S. factories to foreign countries.

Chapter Three

Military

There are a number of prerequisites required to insure the ongoing security and military superiority of the United States. The absence of any one or more of these prerequisites greatly impacts the ability of our military forces to prevail in a conflict. The prerequisites are; a strong military force, a battle strategy for the future, an unrestricted warfare policy, home front support and adequate personnel availability.

STRONG MILITARY FORCE

On December 7, 1941 the United States experienced tremendous losses at Pearl Harbor because of our acquiesce with the world community on matters concerning the security of the United States.

In 1922 the United States under the leadership of President Warren Harding joined with an international tribunal that agreed on how best to preserve world peace. The Washington Naval Treaty had severe impact upon the U.S. Navy as it virtually emasculated our building of a modern fleet. The treaty was particularly relevant during this period as the state of a nations fighting capability was measured by the strength of their navy and specifically by their number of combat ready battleships.

The Washington Naval Treaty required that the United States destroy a number of older vessels including the battleships Michigan and South Carolina. The major impact of the treaty upon the United States was the requirement that the U.S. discontinue the planning, designing and building of modern battleships. The battleships Washington, South Dakota, Indiana, Montana , North Carolina, Iowa and Massachusetts were either under construction or planned at the time the treaty was signed. Those battleships under construction were scrapped and the plans for the remaining were terminated.

In 1930 the United States agreed at the London Naval Disarmament Conference to further deplete our fleet by demilitarizing the battleships Utah and Wyoming. The U.S. remained in a holding pattern on the building of battleships from 1923 to 1939 while the Japanese and Germans continued unabated in the building of modern warships. Finally the keel of the North Carolina was laid in 1939 and it was launched on November of 1941, which was just in time for World War II.

Our non-militaristic mindset and lack of a meaningful military presence prior to 1941 literally invited Japan to attack Pearl Harbor. If we had maintained a strong military presence it is doubtful the Japanese would have brought the U.S. into their war of expansionism. The flawed policy of our government led the United States into World War II and the war cost us the lives of 407,317 military personnel, wounded amounting to 671,846 and the eventual mobilization of 16,353,659 personnel. In addition to the human toll the U.S. spent untold millions upon war materials for our troops and those of our allies. It required several years of intense struggle both on the battlefield and on the home front for the United States to assemble the might necessary to defeat the Axis forces.

History has proven that the United States can never allow our military forces to be anything less than a mighty force. During World War II it was evident to all citizens of the United States that we were involved in a war that could impact our very freedom. History has also vividly illustrated that diplomatic solutions and disarmament treaties based upon the actions of a world body are never to be trusted as a substitute for the security and well being of the United States.

The International Institute of Strategic Studies provided the following statistics concerning major military forces:

NATIONS WITH LARGEST ARMED FORCES

COUNTRY	MILITARY PERSONNEL*	ANNUAL BUDGET
United States	2,692,000	$347,900,000,000
China	2,270,900	$47,000,000,000
India	1,833,000	$4,300,000,000
N. Korea	5,782,000	$2,100,000,000
Pakistan	1,133,000	$2,400,000,000
Russia	3,388,000	$65,000,000,000
S. Korea	5,186,000	$11,400,000,000

Iran	870,000	$4,800,000,000
Vietnam	3,484,000	$2,400,000,000
Germany	686,000	$27,500,000,000
France	360,000	$33,600,000,000
Japan	287,000	$40,300,000,000
UK	467,000	$35,400,000,000

* Military personnel figures include both active and reserve forces.

WEAPONS

COUNTRY	WARSHIPS/ CARRIERS	SUBS	PLANES	NUCLEAR
United States	129/12	72	3136	Yes
China	63/0	69	1900	Yes
India	27/1	16	701	Yes
N. Korea	3/0	26	621	Yes
Pakistan	8/0	10	366	Yes
Russia	32/1	53	1736	Yes
S. Korea	39/0	20	538	No
Iran	3/0	6	386	No
Vietnam	6/0	2	189	No
Germany	14/0	14	446	No
France	35/1	10	449	Yes

Japan	16	16	280	No
United Kingdom	35/3	16	332	Yes

The statistics indicate that the United States remains the dominant world power primarily because we have the ability to dominate the open seas with an extensive fleet based around twelve aircraft carriers brisling with aircraft. The carriers are very significant as they represent the ability to rapidly reposition twelve military bases around the world at our discretion. Our battle readiness is more problematic under the sea as other nations have in their fleets a substantial number of submarines. It is likely many of these are obsolete diesel powered boats, however, the United States should make absolutely certain that we continue to closely monitor the positions of the sub fleets around the world. The United States Navy has the most advanced detection, tracking and undersea military hardware. It is imperative that we continue the development of even more sophisticated equipment as we must maintain the capability to locate and destroy enemy submarines. As to military personnel; our forces are highly trained; however, the total number of our military personnel is not overpowering when compared with the land forces of other nations.

FUTURE BATTLE STRATEGY

Winning a conventional war has always required that the enemy land be taken and occupied by ground troops. Traditionally, the loser surrenders, fighting ceases and the victors occupy the land. Conquered lands were occupied and controlled by aggressors or saviors depending upon different viewpoints. The victors imposed their wishes, religious beliefs or political philosophy upon the defeated populace and time moved forward.

The rules of combat have changed within the last few years as demonstrated by our experiences with the religious extremists of Afghanistan and Iraq. The United States ground forces have been using a tactic of win-hold-win which means that the forces will conquer an area, hold that area and move on to conquer another area. Logically, when you are liberating a people that have been brutalized it is normal to believe that the war is over when the last area has been liberated.

Unfortunately, we are dealing with a mentality that is so immersed in fanaticism and preservation of despotic control of the population that logic does not prevail. Obviously substantial numbers of the populations are not motivated sufficiently to move from a government controlled by religious zealots and demagogues to a democratic form of government. The fanatical mindset of these people is based upon blind religious convictions, revenge, ignorance, poverty and a complete lack of human rights. Collectively these factors create a never-ending pattern of despair and trauma.

The way of this region of the world is beyond the comprehension of the people of the United States and we are not in position to effectively change a life style that has been in existence for centuries.

Their leaders obviously have a focused agenda that includes maintaining a power base with little regard to peace, education, democracy, preservation of life, human rights and the pursuit of health and happiness. It will require the desire and action of the people of Afghanistan and Iraq to change their government and their way of life. If they do not have the will to do so then their plight is self-induced and should remain their problem.

Afghanistan and Iraq represent only two of the nations of the world that prefers governments intertwined with religion. A summary of those nations with substantial Muslim populations follows. The purpose of this list is to illustrate the unlikely but potentially dangerous logistics of pursuing a religious based world wide conflict that would involve Muslims from many nations.

Many of the nations are responsible nations with stable governments, enlightened leaders and economies that are prospering. The United States has an excellent working relationship with most of these nations and it is hoped that the United States and the responsible nations of the Muslim world can together forge a path that will insure mutual existence with peace and harmony.

Others remain in the dark ages and because of their uncivilized suicide attacks and unrelenting warlike attitude they remain a military threat to the United States, their Muslim neighbors and other peace loving nations of the world:

MAJOR MUSLIM NATIONS

NATION	POPULATION	% MUSLIM
Afghanistan	27,756,000	98.1
Algeria	31,261,000	99.7
Egypt	66,341,000	89.
Indonesia	211,023,000	76.5
Iran	65,457,000	95.6
Iraq	24,002,000	96.
Jordan	5,260,000	93.5
Libya	5,369,000	97.
Niger	10,640,000	90.7
Pakistan	145,960,000	96.1
Saudi Arabia	23,370,000	93.3
Senega	19,905,000	92.
Somalia	7,753,000	99.9
Syria	17,156,000	86.
Tunisia	9,764,000	98.9
Yemen	19,495,000	99.9

Included in the above summary are a number of African nations. Africa experiences a different set of problems than the far east. An acquaintance has had over forty years of experience of living and working in many nations of Africa. First, he worked as a Peace

Corps volunteer and later he worked with most of the African nations as a resident specialist affiliated with a major international agency. His comments, based upon an entire career, relate that with the exception of a few nations the majority of African nations still operate under the rule of tribal warfare. Unfortunate as it may be, the role of civilized nations in Africa has been limited to supplying modern weapons for fanning the flames of revelation and the continuation of tribal warfare.

It is questionable that the United States has the time, funds, personnel and patience to change the century upon century traditions of self-government by warlords, tyrants and religious zealots. The United States and its people have little in common with the people of the barbaric nations and it is time to reconsider our worldwide commitment to police the world.

An option for consideration is that we avoid conflicts with these nations unless they clearly committed an act of serious aggression against the United States or our people. If conflict is unavoidable, then our military should replace the traditional "take and occupy" tactic with one of "containment and retribution". Containment could be accomplished by our naval forces, aircraft and minimal numbers of liaison troops. Depending upon the severity of the actions taken against the United States we should apply retribution at whatever level necessary to make all enemies fully understand that "Do not even think of attacking the United of America". Retribution should be retribution and the funding and logistics of the rebuilding process within the aggressor nation should be the problem of that nation.

UNRESTRICTED WARFARE

During the Korean conflict the term "limited warfare" was born. Our troops were faced with massive numbers of Chinese troops and our military forces were not allowed to attack the enemy at the avenues of entry from China to North Korea. President Truman and General Douglas McArthur disagreed to the point that the General was removed from command. It was only through the valiant efforts of U.S. troops that the North Koreans were held in check and there they remain fifty years later behind the 38th parallel.

In Vietnam, the term "limited warfare" again became a deterrent for our troops. Permission was never given to allow unlimited air and naval attacks upon Hanoi. The lack of aggressive action by our forces allowed the forces of North Vietnam to gather strength and eventually prevail on the battlefield. Ironically, the U.S. had the naval and air power to obliterate Hanoi from which all equipment, munitions and power flowed to their troops in the jungles to the South.

Both Korea and Vietnam were examples of unlimited warfare used in a geographic sense. Somewhere in the future the United States will be locked in a combat situation with a major power that has massive numbers of troops and ground support equipment that surpass our logistical capability. Should this unthinkable situation ever arise it is only right that our troops should ultimately have the authority of use all of the weapons within our arsenal including low yield tactical nuclear weapons. Philosophically, war at the front lines is no different than a one-on-one confrontation in a dark alley with an armed and dangerous assailant. The battle in the alley and combat in the battlefield both reduce to the smallest common denominator of "kill or be killed". It is the responsibility of our government and military command to put the rest of the nations on notice that the United States will protect itself and it military personnel with all of the power we have and hold with little regard to political influences.

HOME FRONT SUPPORT

During World War I and II the citizens of the United States firmly supported the actions of our government and our fighting forces. In both cases there was a strong patriotic surge because all were aware that losing the war and our way of life as Americans was not an option. Home front support was very intense during World War II from school children, to the women making war material, to the titans of industry. It was a war we could not lose.

In contrast, the efforts of our troops in Vietnam were impacted by the lack of home front support. Iraq is becoming an increasingly volatile political issue. The history of modern day United States indicates that there are several reasons that home front support is problematic in conflicts:

1. Lack of patriotism.

2. Disagreement with governmental policies and actions.

3. Disinterest.

4. Fear of military service.

5. Personal priorities.

It is apparent from our experiences in Vietnam that the citizens of the United States are going to increasingly oppose military actions that do not directly impact the United States and our security. We can feel compassion if tribal warfare breaks out in Africa or a despot rules with savage intent in the far east, but from a practical standpoint the United States can no longer be responsible for over six billion people throughout the world.

If the United States focuses exclusively upon those conflicts that directly impact and threaten our nation and people then overwhelming support of the people is assured.

ADEQUATE PERSONNEL AVAILABILITY

The availability of adequate military personnel is a function of our population, military deployments, enlistments, draft policies and most importantly the overall logistical capability of the enemy. Following is a chart that compares a few of the larger and most populous nations:

COMPARISON OF LARGEST NATIONS

NATIONS	POPULATION	LAND SIZE (SQ. MILES)
United States	290,000,000	3,675,031
China	1,284,211,000	3,696,100
India	1,047,671,000	1,222,559
Russia	143,673,000	6,592,800

Logistically, the above nations are so massive in size and population that it is obvious that the United States could never consider a traditional war with any of the group. The United States possesses the weaponry and trained personnel to prevail over all others in a traditional battle scenario providing the conflict is limited in time and that our military has the option of using all of the weapons in our arsenal. Unfortunately, occupation, the last step of a war, is not a viable option with most of the major nations as the United States does not have the population to provide the ground troops necessary to successfully hold the conquered land. Under prevailing military strategy a war can never be finalized without the possibility of seizing and occupying enemy ground.

Fortunately, oceans protect the United States and the extensive distances provide response time. The United States has a naval advantage and as long as we maintain absolute superiority on the seas we can prevent the transportation of enemy troops to the shores of the United States. It is possible for enemies to ravage a continent, but we have the power to make sure they never land upon the shores of the United States. To reinforce my views of a "continental containment" defense posture I have inserted quotes from Sun Tzu, a Chinese warrior-philosopher. He wrote the *Art of War* over two thousand years ago and according to a translation by Thomas Cleary, he said:

" If you are fewer, then keep away if you are able".

and

" Invincibility is a matter of defense, vulnerability is a matter of attack".

MILITARY DEPLOYMENT

Following are the approximate numbers of deployed troops as of early 2004. The numbers are changing daily on Iraq; however, these statistics offer a broad view for our commitments:

DEPLOYMENT SITES

COUNTRY	ACTIVE TROOPS	RESERVES/NATL GUARD
Afghanistan	9,600	--
Germany	68,000	_
Iraq	41,000	79,000
Italy	13,000	--
Japan	54,700 *	--
South Korea	38,700	--
United Kingdom	5,700	--
	230,700	79,000

* In addition to the military personnel listed the U.S. has 185 combat aircraft stationed in Japan along with their crews.

In keeping with my preference of national defense as compared to a worldwide offense there are comments that are appropriate for consideration:

Afghanistan ----- Remove all of troops as quickly as feasible.

Germany---------As reported in the *Los Angeles Times* our military is already removing troops from Germany and relocating to Hungry, Poland, Romania and Bulgaria. Their logic is that we no longer need to guard the "old Europe" and that troops and equipment will be much nearer port facilities for a more speedy deployment.

Iraq ----------- We need to let the Iraqis fight their own battles and bring all of our troops home as soon as we have turned the government over to the newly formed Iraq government.

Italy ----------Why do we have 13,000 troops in Italy? Bring them home.

Japan --------Japan has Japanese armed forces amounting to 287,000 and they spend over forty billion dollars a year on their military. Japan is not a country in need financially or militarily. They have a population of over 127,000,000, a household income of about $61,000 which is almost twenty thousand dollars more than the average U.S. household. They have a national debt that is about $2,500,000,000,000 compared to the U.S. national debt of over $7,000,000,000,000. Bring home the troops.

South Korea - For over fifty years the United States has had a major presence in this nation for the sole purpose of protecting them against the North Koreans. The facts show that they like Japan are most self-sufficient. They have a population of about 48,000,000 which compares to the about 23,000,000 in North Korea. Their average household income exceeds the U.S. figure by about $4,000 annually, and they have a national debt of about $47,000,000,000, which compares to the U.S. national debt of over $7, 000,000,000,000. Bring home the troops.

UK ----------- We have about 5,000 military personnel in the United Kingdom. I am comfortable with this deployment as they are our best ally and the U.K. is strategically located at the gateway to Europe

RETENTION OF TROOPS

Rand Research did an extensive study of the impact of deployments as to the reenlistment of enlisted personnel and officer retention. They found that the number of deployments over the last few years has risen sharply. In one case the Marine Corps performed fifteen contingency operations from 1982 to 1989. Since 1989 they have performed over sixty contingency operations. Rand concluded that deployments had little effect upon the reenlistments and retentions.

RECRUITING

According to the U.S. Army Recruiting Command the enlistment of recruits has been affected by the mini wars and deployments of the last few years. Following is a chart showing the comparisons:

YEAR	ACTIVE ARMY	RESERVES
1990	88,600	57,400
2003	74,100	27,400

It is apparent that all recruiting has suffered recently, specifically reserve enlistments.

SUMMARY

Our normal battle tactic of win-hold-win does not apply in the fanatical wars of today and we need to reconsider "holding land". We as a nation do not have the population to battle with the most populous nations of the world, however, we do have the military might to protect the United States. Our resources are stretched with current deployments and the termination of some deployments should be considered.Deployments do not impact reenlistments or the retention of officers; however, recruiting is problematic.

Chapter Four

Foreign Aid

The term "Foreign Aid" has always been a mystery to most Americans. We are aware that considerable funds are sent to faraway places but it is doubtful that one out of a thousand Americans has little knowledge of the subject. The purpose of this chapter is to present a summary of the programs, inform as to the monetary requirements, to address the distribution of funds and finally to comment upon the validity of the various programs.

Following is a chart indicating our massive increases over recent times and the figures are approximate. Following that are the U.S. Department of State proposed account tables for 2003. These statistics are the latest detailed information that we can obtain as to the distribution of funds, however, they will offer an overview of the nations involved, the various programs and the funds required:

FOREIGN AID BUDGETS

2001	2002	2003	2004
$12,464,373,000	$13,153,639,000	$13,803,109,000	$37,000,000,000 *

* Includes normal budget of $17 billion plus $20 billion for rebuilding Iraq.

U.S. DEPARTMENT OF STATE / ACCOUNT TABLES

Development Assistance, Child Survival and Health Programs	$2,739,500,000
Economic Support Fund	2,290,000,000
Assistance for Eastern Europe and the Baltic States	495,000,000
Assistance for the Independent States of the Former Soviet Union	755,000,000
International Narcotics Control and Law Enforcement	928,000,000
Nonproliferation, Anti-terrorism, Demining, and Related Programs	372,400,000
International Military Education and Training	80,000,000
Foreign Military Financing	4,107,200,000
Peacekeeping Operations / Contributions to Peacekeeping Activities	834,231,000
International Organizations and Programs & Contributions	1,201,778,000
	_____
TOTAL	$13,803,109,000

The report is nineteen pages long and I have summarized the mountains of statistics in order that readers may more easily grasp the overall significance of the report. The following categories, A through E include all of the various budgetary items from the report in a consolidated format. I eliminated nations or line items that were receiving less than $5,000,000 in benefits. Following are the nations and proposed funds:

A -- Development Assistance/Health Programs

B -- Economic Support Fund, Assistance for Eastern Europe, Baltic States and Independent States of the former Soviet Union.

C -- International Narcotics Control, Nonproliferation and Anti-Terrorism.

D -- International Military Education and Training, Foreign Military Financing and Peacekeeping Operations and Contributions for Peacekeeping Operations.

E -- International Organizations and Programs, Contributions to International Organizations.

($ in thousands)

NATIONS	A	B	C	D	E
INTERNATIONAL					
United Nations					279,327
World Health Org.					93,616
UN Development					100,000
UN Children's Fund					120,000
Other				595,600	583,235
AFRICA					
Angola	7,400				
Benin	12,261				
Congo	21,500			273,226	
Ethiopia				55,594	
Eritrea	8,519				
Ghana	39,743				
Guinea	20,725				
Kenya	46,693				
Liberia	5,200				
Madagascar	17,528				
Malawi	30,877				

Mali	32,961			
Mozambique	45,492			
Namibia	5,480			
Nigeria	66,235			12,800
Rwanda	18,173			12,500
Senegal	28,380			
Sierra Leone	3,868			145,803
South Africa	62,428		7,450	6,000
Sudan	22,300			
Tanzania	32,936			
Uganda	62,944			
Zambia	50,285			
Zimbabwe	18,108			
Regional	135,061	32,000	7,000	34,500
EAST ASIA PACIFIC				
Burma	6,500			
Cambodia	22,500	17,000		
China		5,000		
East Timor	19,000	65,177		
Indonesia	71,472	60,000		
Mongolia	12,000			
Philippines	50,659	20,000		22,400

Thailand	3,250		3,750	3,750
Vietnam	12,465			
SOUTH ASIA				
Afghanistan	n/a			n/a
Bangladesh	57,220	7,000		
India	75,185	25,000		51,000
Nepal	31,696	6,000		
Pakistan	50,000	200,000	4,000	51,000
Sri Lanka	6,050	4,000		
Regional	74,547	11,250	96,063	
So. Pacific Fisheries			18,000	
NEAR EAST				
Egypt		615,000		1,301,200
Golan Heights				8,365
Iraq	n/a			n/a
Israel		600,000		2,100,000
Iraq Opposition		25,000		
Jordan		250,000		200,400
Lebanon		32,000		33,520
Morocco		6,713		6,500

Oman		20,000
Tunisia		6,500
West Bank/ Gaza	75,000	
Western Sahara		11,792
Yemen	10,000	
Region	82,297	
EUROPE & EURASIA		
Albania	28,000	
Armenia	70,000	
Azerbaijan	46,000	
Belarus	9,500	
Bosnia	50,000	20,000
Bulgaria	28,000	10,085
Croatia	30,000	8,300
Czech Republic		12,900
Estonia		7,850
Georgia	87,000	14,716
Hungary		12,900
Kazakhstan	43,000	4,000
Kosovo	85,000	109,034

Kyrgyzstan		36,000		5,100
Latvia				8,100
Lithuania				8,600
Macedonia		50,000		11,000
Moldova		32,500		
Montenegro		25,000		
Poland				15,000
Romania		29,000		11,500
Russia		148,000		
Serbia		110,000		
Slovakia				9,000
Tajikistan		7,000		
Turkey				19,800
Ukraine		155,000		5,700
Uzbekistan		31,500		9,950
Yugoslavia		135,000		16,656
Regional		194,000		
WESTERN				
Bahamas			12,000	
Bolivia	30,547	10,000	91,000	
Brazil	17,537		12,000	
Caribbean	15,570			7,130
Colombia			439,000	99,180

Cuba		6,000		
Dominican Rep.	19,409			
Ecuador	7,130	22,250	37,000	
El Salvador	33,724			
Guatemala	26,691	7,500		
Haiti	25,000			
Honduras	35,096			
Jamaica	13,180			
Mexico	18,276	12,000	12,000	
Nicaragua	27,258			
Panama	7,000	3,500	9,000	
Paraguay	6,625	3,500		
Peru	26,927	12,250	135,000	
Venezuela			8,000	
Regional	90,001	4,000	9,500	
EUROPE				
Cyprus		15,000		5,219
Ireland		29,000		
Regional				14,550

SUMMARY

From a humanitarian viewpoint, The Development Assistance, Child Survival and Health Program line item warrants the most consideration. The Economic Support and Assistance funds are a lesser priority as the United States could likely present a strong case that we require more economic support than most of the recipients. Narcotics Control is currently necessary but the real answer is control of our citizens, not the foreign manufacturing and distribution of narcotics. The International Organizations and Programs and Contributions line item budget is equally necessary and repugnant as it represents government bureaucracy out of control.

The most controversial line item is the International Military Education and Training, Foreign Military Financing, Peacekeeping Operations and Contributions to Peacekeeping. I find this a dichotomy, as we provide funds to many of the nations in the world for both combat training and the financing of military equipment. On the other hand, when nations do battle we send in the troops to terminate the military action, pay for the peacekeeping operations and usually rebuild the areas of conflict. I wish I could say that we should cease all military aid and let the nations of the world fund their own military options, both war and peace. I believe this philosophy could apply to most nations of the world.

Unfortunately, it appears that the Middle East is going to remain a volatile battleground environment forever. The United States has traditionally been providing about 20% of our annual foreign aid budget to Israel. I question the validity of economic support to Israel, however, I do support our military contributions to Israel, as they provide an important military counterbalance within the Middle East.

Chapter Five

Health Care

The United States Health care system is ranked number thirty-seven by the World Health Organization. We have a problem and it is shared by millions of our citizens expressing concern about their care. Following is a focused view of this highly controversial issue and a report from The World Health Organization for the year 2002. This report is itself controversial as the figures indicate that countries with socialized health care are more efficient and cost effective than the U.S. free enterprise system. However, socialized medicine is not necessarily the answer and commentaries on health care follow by country. The following charts on health care indicators and costs provide an overview of the current status of the United States as to several industrialized nations:

HEALTH CARE INDICATORS

NATION	LIFE EXPECTANCY		INFANT MORTALITY	PERSONS PER DOCTOR
	Male	Female	@ 1000 births	
United States	74.6	79.8	9.7	360
Australia	77.9	83.	6.5	400
Canada	77.2	82.3	6.5	540
France	75.9	83.5	5.4	330

Germany	75.6	81.6	5.4	290
Italy	76.8	82.5	5.5	180
Japan	78.4	85.3	4.4	530
Switzerland	77.7	83.3	6.5	260
United Kingdom	75.8	80.5	7.6	720

COST OF HEALTH CARE

NATION	COST PER CAPITA (Per person)	% OF GDP (Gross Domestic Product)
United States	$4,887	13.9
Australia	2,532	9.2
Canada	2,792	9.5
France	2,567	9.6
Germany	2,820	10.8
Italy	2,204	8.4
Japan	2,231	8.0
Switzerland	3,322	11.
United Kingdom	1,989	7.6

The Commonwealth Fund of New York City, which is a private foundation supporting research of health and social issues, did a study in 2002 on a few nations as to access problems of patients based upon cost. They found that cost is a factor and following are some of the results based upon percentages:

PERCENT OF ACCESS PROBLEMS COST RELATED

	UK	AUST.	CANADA	U.S.
Did not fill prescription	7	19	13	26
Had a medical problem but did not visit doctor	3	11	5	24
Did not get test, treatment or follow up	2	15	6	22

UNITED STATES

Under our current system we have over 43,000,000 citizens that for one reason or another are not covered by medical insurance. This number will continue to rise as many companies are eliminating their paid medical insurance programs to employees or requiring more employee participation in paying for the insurance. In addition to the uninsured we have a problem of access as shown above.

Our medical cost continues to rise astronomically and one explanation as voiced by the health care industry follows. Medical facilities that participate with the federally administered Medicare program or the federally funded Medicaid program must give free care to all that approach their emergency facilities. These services provided to non-paying patients reduce the profit of the facility. As our medical facilities are profit centers they respond by raising the costs to offset the losses caused by non-paying patients. These increased costs are passed along to patients with medical insurance and the increases are ultimately included in insurance premiums. In essence those with medical insurance are providing health care for those who do not have insurance.

Another problem is that those who pay nothing take advantage of the system. A doctor friend of mine who worked in emergency services related to me that it is common for relatives to bring older patients to the facility so they might leave town for a few days.

The New Bureau, from the University of Illinois reported the following from data analyzed by Tom O'Rourke, professor of community health at the University of Illinois and Nicholas Lammarino, professor of kinesiology at Rice University:

1. U.S. health-care administrative costs are 60 percent higher than in Canada and 97 percent higher than in the United Kingdom.
2. There is no evidence to suggest that significantly higher health-care expenditures are associated with either better outcomes or improved health status.
3. U.S. health care costs continue to be far higher and have risen more rapidly than other nations.

A doctor friend who has practiced for many years in the geriatrics field of medicine (diseases of the aged) advises that a substantial portion of our medical expenditures are spent during the last days of the lives of our older people. On a regular basis he sees aged patients without a living will kept alive for a brief period of time due to heroic measures requested by the family. My friend has two concerns; one is the inordinate expense of sustaining life on a very temporary basis and two, the patients right to die in peace.

Malpractice insurance has become the scourge of the medical profession. The premiums paid by the doctors and hospitals is expensive and as in any business the cost must be passed along to the customers. Unfortunately, the legal profession with advertising combined with unrealistic awards by jurors have accelerated the law suit process. The United States has become a very litigious society and the cost is ultimately being borne by all of our citizens.

Following are brief summaries of the health care plans of nations that appeared on the health care indicator report. A point to consider in the comparison is that a number of these nations have homogenous populations with similar mindsets. In contrast, the United States is a potpourri of races and creeds with differing views and responses to health care and preventative measures.

AUSTRALIA

Australia has a care system divided between the public and private sectors. All Australians have Medicare, which is funded by a tax upon income. It provides free treatment in public hospitals and free or subsidized medical treatment by practitioners, specialists and participating optometrists. The program includes a subsidized list of prescription medicines. Private Health Insurance is available for those who wish to have a choice of doctors, reduced waiting times on surgery plus other advantages.

On an Internet site, backed by the University of Sydney, well-directed comments were made by Vern Hughes concerning the problems with the Australian health care system. His report makes these points:

1. Medicare remains very popular and demand exceeds capabilities.
2. Private insurers can not keep costs from rising.
3. Private insurers are having problems in expanding memberships.
4. Medicare is not structured to contain costs.
5. Doctors are paid on a fee-for-service basis with no incentives for collaborating with others.
6. Fee-for-service compensation promotes over-servicing and discourages preventative care.

Mr. Hughes recommends integrated health care, which is a partnership between health insurance suppliers and community membership-based organizations. This partnership according to him will be in position to negotiate and present to members cost effective procedures, which will hopefully create more patient capacity and maintain costs. His plan sounds similar to our HMO programs.

CANADA

Canada has a predominantly publicly financed health care system. Their aim is that all eligible residents have reasonable access to medical services on a prepaid basis, without direct charges at the point of service. As per the statistics above they do provide a reasonable level of health care treatment. However, in response to a 2002 survey performed by The Commonwealth Fund two thirds of those surveyed advised they were dissatisfied with the current Canadian Health Care Program. Those surveyed advised that their three biggest problems were:

1. Shortages of health professionals or hospital beds.
2. Long waiting lines.
3. Delay of scheduled surgery or procedure due to cancellation.

The dissatisfied Canadians recommended that their government should spend more money to correct the problems.

FRANCE

France is ranked number one by the World Health Organization. Everyone working in France must contribute to the French Social Security system and everyone is entitled to benefit from it with no exceptions. Contributions are made by employers and employees to fund the program and payroll taxes amount to 12.8% of total wages with 6.8% deducted from the employee. This payment only covers the Health System and they have other payroll deductions for the Family System (day care, maternity leave, etc,) and for the Retirement System. Patients control their own medical records and they can visit any doctor or dentist of their choice including specialists. Minor medical advice may be given by their pharmacist. When they visit they pay the doctor directly and are later reimbursed by the government health plan. Doctor and dental appointments for non-life-threatening problems are reimbursed at 80% and prescription reimbursements vary. Serious illnesses, including those of old age, are covered 100%.

Early in 2004 Jacques Chirac, the president of France, was quoted in an article that appeared in the *Washington Times.com*. He stated that France's health care system was sick and broke. The article went on to say that the plan is 14 billion dollars in debt with estimates of a deficit in 2020 of 132 billion dollars. Public confidence in the system has waned due to the many deaths that occurred during the heat of the summer of 2003. The Chirac article concluded by his recommendation that the government must pursue radical changes in the health care system and that there must be a competitive plan between the private and public sectors.

GERMANY

The health care system of Germany provides its residents with nearly universal access to quality medical care through a choice of physicians. Approximately 90% of the population receives health care through the statutory health care insurance program. Membership and insurance premiums are compulsory for all those earning less than a periodically revised income ceiling. The remaining 10% of the population with high incomes purchase private insurance. Both groups use the same health care facilities.

According to Professor Dr. Stefan Felder of the Institute of Social Medicine at the University of Magdeburg changes are urgently required in the current system. He lists the following problems:

1. The system has extensive regulations that need to be simplified.

2. The services are performed with no cost to patients which lead to excess demand.

Dr. Felder believes that the inclusion of co-payments is very important as a control factor for patient over demand. His recommendation is that the German program be changed using Switzerland's health care program as a model and the Swiss plan follows:

SWITZERLAND

The Swiss do not have a centralized health care system. Individual cantons (states) are responsible for determining the levels of service, administering and delivering the services. The Swiss plan requires that all citizens must purchase the basic health care plan and at their option purchase private insurance to receive extra services and improved medical facilities. Subsidies are available for those with low incomes. Most hospitals in Switzerland are public institutions that receive public funding. There are also about 100 private hospitals that receive little or no public funding.

The Swiss plan utilizes several levels of deductibles, which may be selected by the purchaser of the basic plan. If a person is in good health he might opt for a higher deductible and a correspondingly lower insurance premium. If the person is in poor health he might opt for a low deductible because of his increased medical visits.

Approximately 70% of the cost of a visit to a physician is covered by insurance and 30% by the patient. As a result most Swiss families spend about 10% of their budget of medical related services and insurance.

ITALY

The Italian National Health Service covers all Italians. The plan provides free service to all citizens subject to co-payments covering about three percent of the total expenditure. The plan is financed by general taxation.

Italy has a relatively efficient health care compared with the other Organization for Economic Co-operation and Development (OECD) nations. This efficiency is attributed to a high degree of decentralization; however, the success of the health plan could be partially responsible to the Mediterranean diet of the Italian people.

However, according to a report by the International Monetary Fund, all is not perfect in Italy. The IMF report mentions these problems:

1. Patients are experiencing long waits for diagnostic tests and hospitalization.

2. Italian health care costs are rising more quickly than their Gross Domestic Product which actually is true of all of the OECD nations.

3. The Italian central government does not do an acceptable job of distributing health care equipment and funds and the local health officials are not accountable.

4. The cost of medical supplies and equipment is excessive compared with other national averages due in some part to excessive delays in payments to suppliers.

5. Weak accounting practices, lack of professional management personnel and the lack of safeguards to ensure that bribery from suppliers does not contaminate the purchasing process.

JAPAN

Japan's medical services are provided by a public mandatory insurance program, which is run by two systems: occupation-based and region-based. The occupation-based system includes employees of companies, government employees, teachers and seamen. All citizens that are not included in the occupation-based system are included in the region-based system. Both systems are financed by premiums (56.1%), subsidy from the general budget (32%) and co-payments from patients (11.9%). They also have a long-term care program, which is financed by a 50% tax and contributions of 50%. The contributions are collected from adults age 40 and over plus co-payments of 10% of costs of care.

Japan's Ministry of Health and Welfare oversees the socialized program and Neil Weinberg in *Forbes* wrote in an article that tight monetary controls by the Ministry have impacted the level of services and have caused anomalies within the system. Consultation fees are kept unrealistically low per office visit and doctors look for compensation elsewhere. One of their options is to own a small hospital which grossly extends the time spent in the hospital by patients. Another income producing ploy is to over prescribe drugs with inflated prices. As to procedures, surgeons complain that the health ministry will not let them import the latest medical devices in an attempt to hold down prices within the health care system.

UNITED KINGDOM

The National Health Service is responsible for health care in the UK. It is a nationally administered, centralized service that is financed from tax dollars. The NHS works on the principle that there is a right to be registered with a general practitioner, and the right to be medically examined. There is no formal right to receive any treatment or care upon demand.

Over 70% of the NHS funds goes to hospitals and the general practice receives about 10% of the funds even though they deal with approximately 95% of the reported medical problems.

The Commonwealth Fund on international health policy found that 60% of U.K. survey participants advised that the NHS system required a complete overhaul. The survey indicated that the doctors were rated either excellent or very good. Hospital ratings did not fare as well and 22% rated care as fair or poor. Waiting times for access to specialists and for procedures was by far the most valid concern. Over one-third of the participants advised it is difficult to see a specialist and that same number reported waits of four months for non-emergency surgery.

SUMMARY

It is obvious the United States must make improvements in health care. We have the most renowned medical professionals in the world, the most prestigious medical facilities and millions of highly intelligent people capable of addressing the issue. According to the world norms we are spending more now that we should be for health care. We must address coverage for those who do not have insurance as in effect we are already paying the bill now for uncontrolled care at inflated prices. Our cost of health care administration is absolutely ridiculous and should be completely rethought and restructured.

The United States can do wonders if the medical profession, the drug companies, the government and the patients all make a dedicated, unselfish effort to seriously address the problems. We have the ability to improve the service and lower costs if we will just do it.

Following are a wide range of simplistic suggestions for consideration. Several of the suggestions were developed in response to the problems encountered by other nations. Others were developed in the spirit of brainstorming:

1. The health care administration costs of the U.S. are astronomically high and we must eliminate the endless nightmare and ambiguities of billing concerns that completely dominate the health care system.

    Each medical service provider now bills patients at inflated prices knowing that the bill will be paid in reduced amounts from several sources. Those sources include a co-pay from the patient, private insurance, Medicare or Medicaid. I recommend that bills for actual amounts due be sent by the medical service providers to those responsible for payment. One software system could be developed for all medical service providers who participate with Medicare and Medicaid. The software would include preset reimbursements for all procedures from either the government and or the patient's private insurer as selected from a data bank including all insurers.

2. This came from the French --- allow pharmacists to give limited advice and prescribe low risk medication for minor health problems.

3. And from the Germans and Swiss --- meaningful co-pays are absolutely necessary to control patient over demand.

4. Place a cap on malpractice court awards --- also encourage the private insurance sector to offer supplemental malpractice policies for consumers who wish to have additional protection against malpractice.

5. From Switzerland --- encourage private hospitals, clinics and doctors to provide care exclusively for those patients with private insurance or adequate funding.

6. Require substantial patient co-pays for heroic procedures that are not based upon sound medical judgment within the field of geriatrics.

Some of the above suggestions are truly controversial, however, the purpose of this book is provide information on problematic areas, compare with other nations for insight and develop a wide range of ideas for consideration.

Chapter Six

Social Security

Controversy has been brewing over the financial status of our Social Security System. Some in Washington believe the Social Security Fund will run out of funds in the future if we do not make some serious adjustments. Others believe the system is properly funded. One thing is for certain:

The population of the United States is getting older and there are less workers in proportion contributing to Social Security!

Younger workers are concerned that the funds they contribute over the years will not be available at their retirement age. They also are concerned that the retirement age will be extended to an unreasonable time due to a lack of funds. Older citizens worry that their Social Security checks will be reduced or terminated. All citizens are aware that the program must be addressed and the question is how do we accomplish the feat in a manner that is truly fair and acceptable to all. Following are a couple of recommendations addressing the current program and those comments will be followed by a plan for consideration.

I envisioned the major purpose of the Social Security Program as one of providing a retirement program for older citizens. I was surprised to learn that the Public Assistance and Welfare Services Program is an integral part of Social Security. This program includes aid to needy families with children, medical assistance, maternal and child health service, family and child welfare services, food stamps and energy assistance.

In public discussions the fact that social security funds are also being used for welfare is not being brought to focus. I believe these two agendas are entirely different in the eyes of most people. The two should be separate in funding; one being retirement and the other welfare.

Social Security is vulnerable to fraud through multiple filings by individuals. I recommend that a very tough program be initiated to recover funds along with a plan to eliminate multiple payments. One method for consideration would be a national data bank on each citizen complete with positive identification such as fingerprints.

A positive factor is the growth of personal IRA accounts, as they will contribute to the financial well being of retired people. Social Security was not really designed as a retirement plan but as financial assistance in the very trying days of the great depression. The personal retirement plans of our younger workers should eventually take some of the financial burden off of Social Security:

THE PLAN

My book is an exercise in brainstorming to initiate creative thought for problem solving and following is a hyperextension of that technique. The advantages are:

1. The plan is designed so that contributors are reimbursed on a timely basis for all deposits plus nominal interest.
2. The plan offers additional financial assistance for those who do not meet their retirement goals. Under the plan these payments will be phased out over time.
3. The plan encourages the use of individual IRA accounts.

As to cost savings, it is logical that the reduction of supplemental payments through selective payments plus the initiation of the phasing out process will positively impact Social Security financial demands.

I recommend that Social Security payments should be addressed as coming from two different sources; one, from the contributor's individual account and secondly, from supplemental payments.

INDIVIDUAL ACCOUNT PAYMENTS

Individual accounts would contain all of the deposits made by the contributor or by his employer on his behalf over the years. The account would be totaled annually with nominal interest accrued. At age sixty-five the account would be totaled and monthly payments would be made to the contributor. The account should be structured as an annuity with a nominal interest rate and payments limited to the life of the contributor. The monthly payment would be based upon the balance of the account plus interest and the time in months from age sixty-five to the mortality age (at that time) of the contributor.

SUPPLEMENTAL PAYMENTS

Supplemental payments would be paid to the contributor in addition to the base individual account payments only if the income of the contributor as confirmed by the previous yearly federal tax records indicate a household income lower than a fixed amount. The amount of supplemental payments would be based upon the difference between the individual account payments and an agreed base amount. Following is a phasing schedule, which reduces the amount of supplemental payments based upon the age of the contributor at the inception of the program:

AGE	PLAN PHASE SCHEDULE
60 or more	Pay amounts established under current S.S. program.
51 to 60	Pay individual account payment plus 80% of supplemental.
41 to 50	" " " " " 60% " "
31 to 40	" " " " " 40% " "
21 to 30	" " " " " 20% " "

A number of phrases and terms follow along with explanations. This information should enable the reader to intelligently consider the case study examples that follow:

INDIVIDUAL ACCOUNT

AGE -------------- Age of contributor at inception of the plan.

GENDER --------- Male or Female

BALANCE ------- Total of all deposits plus accrued interest at age 65.

TIME ------------- Difference in months between age 65 and mortality age at that time by gender.

I PAY ------------- Monthly payment for life beginning at age 65.

FORMULA ------- $\underline{Balance + Interest} = I\ Pay$
$\qquad\qquad\qquad Time$

SUPPLEMENTAL PAYMENT

INCOME ---------- Total household income as reported on prior Federal Tax Return.

QUALIFIED ------ To qualify for supplemental payments income must be below an established amount. For the examples I used $20,000 as a base. If income is over this base no supplemental pay may be received. If income is below the base then supplemental payments would be payable.

BASE -------------- Set monthly payment figure. (I used $1200 monthly)

I PAY-------------- Monthly payment from Individual Account.

DIFFERENCE --- Difference between I Pay and Base.

PHASE ------------ Percentages of supplemental payments allowable based upon above Phase Plan Schedule.

S PAY -------------- Monthly payment from Supplemental Account.

FORMULA --------Base - I Pay = Difference x Phase % = S Pay

EXAMPLE A

INDIVIDUAL ACCOUNT

Age	Gender	Balance	Time	I Pay
45	F	$85,000	192	$443

SUPPLEMENTAL

Income	Qualified	Base	I Pay		Difference		Phase		S Pay
$18,000	Yes	$1200	- 443	=	757	x	60%	=	$454

TOTAL SOCIAL SECURITY MONTHLY CHECK = $897

EXAMPLE B

INDIVIDUAL ACCOUNT

Age	Gender	Balance	Time	I Pay
70	(receives payment under prior S.S. program)			

EXAMPLE C

INDIVIDUAL ACCOUNT

Age	Gender	Balance	Time	I Pay
56	M	$160,000	168	$952

SUPPLEMENTAL

Income	Qualified	Base	Payment	Difference	Phase	S Pay
$45,000	No					$0

TOTAL SOCIAL SECURITY MONTHLY CHECK = $952

EXAMPLE D

INDIVIDUAL ACCOUNT

Age	Gender	Balance	Time	I Pay
25	F	$120,000	180	$667

SUPPLEMENTAL

Income	Qualified	Base	I Pay	Difference	Phase	S Pay
$17,500	Yes	$1200	- $667	= $533	x 20%	= $107

TOTAL SOCIAL SECURITY MONTHLY CHECK = $774

EXAMPLE E

INDIVIDUAL ACCOUNT

Age	Gender	Balance	Time	I Pay
31	M	$200,000	156	$1282

SUPPLEMENTAL

Income	Qualified	Base	I Pay	Difference	Phase	S Pay
No	$1200		(I Pay exceeds base)			$0

TOTAL SOCIAL SECURITY MONTHLY CHECK = $1282

I honestly do not know if this plan will help the Social Security funding problem. It does address a number of serious concerns and it would be interesting for a government study to be done to consider the feasibility, benefits, affordability and budget impact.

Chapter Seven

Education

As the world economy becomes more demanding, careers are going to become more difficult to follow and jobs are going to be more scarce within the United States. The basis for employment depends upon a combination of education and training within a field. The United States is a world leader in education and this chapter will compare our system and results with other nations. It will take into consideration some of the most pressing problems in our educational system and offer some ideas for consideration.

The source for the following Pisa Survey is the Organization for Economic Cooperation and Development (OECD). The survey is based upon a survey of over 265,000 fifteen-year students from selected countries. The numbers represent scales of measure with 500 being an average score. As Americans we should not be too alarmed by our moderate positioning in the survey. Concern over international test rankings is felt in our academic world.

Randy Hitz, the Dean of MSC College of Education made this comment "The U.S. is a very large, diverse and complex nation so using a single average score for all students as a basis of comparison can also be misleading". He also went on to say that the differences in scores within the U.S. are far greater overall than the differences between nations. His conclusion is that there are segments of the

U.S. population that are not doing well, however, one on one U.S. most students fair well against all international competition:

PISA SURVEY LITERACY RESULTS

COUNTRY	READING	MATH	SCIENCE
Australia	528	533	528
Canada	534	533	529
France	505	517	500
Germany	484	490	487
Japan	522	557	550
Russia	462	478	460
Switzerland	494	529	496
United Kingdom	523	529	532
United States	504	493	499

A much more realistic guide as to the success of our education program is the number of students that are graduating from high school. Our efforts have been misdirected in trying to raise our measurable levels of education by fractions of points when we have about 27% of our students dropping out of school without a marketable skill.

Following is a graduation rate by state and race as developed by the Manhattan Institute for Policy Research. The purpose of the following report is not to embarrass anyone but to realistically focus upon the issues so that our nation can address and solve the problem:

GRADUATION RATE BY STATE AND RACE

A = All students   C = Latino

B = African American   D = Caucasian

STATE	A	B	C	D
Alabama	62%	52%	33%	69%
Alaska	67	58	58	74
Arizona	59	54	50	70
Arkansas	72	67	48	74
California	68	59	55	78
Colorado	68	55	47	75
Connecticut	75	64	53	79
Delaware	73	64	57	78
District of Columbia	59	55	59	ins
Florida	59	51	52	63
Georgia	54	44	32	61
Hawaii	69	43	66	67
Idaho	78	na	na	na
Illinois	78	57	55	89
Indiana	74	55	55	77
Iowa	93	57	60	95
Kansas	76	54	51	80

Kentucky	71	na	na	na
Louisiana	69	62	70	76
Maine	78	ins	ins	78
Maryland	75	66	70	80
Massachusetts	75	70	51	78
Michigan	75	53	55	79
Minnesota	82	43	53	87
Mississippi	62	58	ins	66
Missouri	75	58	63	78
Montana	83	ins	82	88
Nebraska	85	53	50	90
Nevada	58	49	40	65
New Hampshire	71	na	na	na
New Jersey	75	66	60	86
New Mexico	65	58	58	74
New York	70	51	53	82
North Carolina	63	55	38	68
North Dakota	88	na	na	na
Ohio	77	49	63	82
Oklahoma	74	64	57	78
Oregon	57	49	43	70
Pennsylvania	82	63	56	86
Rhode Island	72	61	51	77
South Carolina	62	na	na	na

South Dakota	80	ins	ins	89
Tennessee	60	44	38	64
Texas	67	59	56	76
Utah	81	na	na	na
Vermont	84	na	na	na
Virginia	74	64	62	78
Washington	70	na	na	na
West Virginia	82	71	ins	82
Wisconsin	85	40	56	92
Wyoming	81	ins	59	84

ins = insufficient student count. na = data not available.

The figures above clearly indicate that the United States has tens of thousands of students that are dropping out of school each year. When a sixteen year old drops out of school a pattern is established that leads to a low income producing potential, a lack of self esteem, idle time and a young person that is susceptible to a life of crime. All nations have substantial numbers of students that are educationally challenged as people naturally have different motivations, interests and abilities. We as a nation have the obligation to target and help these young dropouts because to turn them loose on the streets is doing both them and the United States a great disservice.

Our national educational program and structure offers basically the same twelve-year program for all students. Again, the numbers prove that this program is not working for approximately 27% of our students. For consideration, I believe there is some merit in modifying our basic educational system to include comprehensive vocational training specifically directed at those in the 27% group.

I researched the educational systems of the world and found that the United Kingdom and Germany are the leaders in providing educational joint scholastic/vocational opportunities for their students.

In the United Kingdom they have a compulsory school age of sixteen years. They have infant schools from ages five to seven and junior schools from ages seven to eleven. They have three different categories of schools for ages eleven to sixteen, one is secondary, another is academic secondary and the last is technical secondary. Students based upon their interests and ability are flowed into these three systems. However, at about age fourteen a decision is made jointly by the student, the parents, and school officials as to a logical career direction for the student. In the past the U.K. worked with industries as to placement of those wanting to enter various trades. Recently they have embarked upon a program to provide more vocational training as part of the school curriculum. As part of that program at age fourteen a student may elect not to continue in the study of the classics, such as mathematics, history, science and foreign language.

Germany has a compulsory school age of fifteen years. They offer twelve years of schooling, however, from grade ten forward they offer an extensive vocational program to those who prefer learning a trade. The vocational schools are still part of the educational system with the only difference being their curriculum. The students still receive free tuition, books and materials and they remain a part of the school and may participate in all of the extracurricular functions. Upon completion of the vocational program a certificate of general education is awarded.

SUMMARY

The United States has a shortage of those properly trained in the trades. We need plumbers, electricians, brick masons, truck drivers, sheet metal workers, carpenters, mechanics, equipment operators and more. Concurrently, we have about 27% of our students dropping out of school with little prospect of earning a living wage. It is a win win situation for all to provide alternative educational opportunities for our youth.

Chapter Eight

Crime

According to sociologists crime is caused by a litany of interwoven social problems. Over the years the media and special interest groups have informed others as to the most predominate causes of crime. Educators decry the lack of education, social workers underscore poverty, poor living conditions and unemployment, and the law enforcement agencies blame drugs. In the meantime the criminals, their family, friends and neighbors blame everyone but themselves.

Following is a comparison of several key factors and how they relate to violent crime by state. The factors taken from the U.S. Census Bureau and the U.S. Department of Health, include basic data on poverty, unemployment, education, drug use and population density of blacks and Hispanics. When analyzing you will find anomalies that defy logic, trends that are surprising, factors that are irrelevant and synergisms that the politicians will not address:

CRIME STATISTICS

A = Violent crimes per 100,000 population.

B = Percent of persons below poverty level.

C = Percent of unemployment.

D = Percent of African American population.

E = Percent of Hispanic population.

F = Percent of those without high school diplomas.

G = Ratings 1 (high usage) through 5 (low usage) of illicit drug use by areas.

STATES	A	B	C	D	E	F	G
Median	438	11.9	5.4	11.3	7.8	15.8	3
DC	1633	20.2	6.4	59.9	n/a	18.0	2
SC	822	12.3	6.0	29.9	2.4	19.8	4
FL	770	12.5	5.1	15.8	16.8	16.9	3
MD	770	8.5	4.4	28.2	4.3	14.8	4
NM	740	18.4	5.4	2.24	2.1	20.4	2
TN	717	13.5	5.1	16.6	2.2	21.0	3
LA	662	19.6	6.1	32.9	2.4	22.4	3
NV	638	10.5	5.5	6.9	19.7	17.0	2
IL	621	10.7	6.5	15.2	12.3	16.0	3
DE	599	9.2	4.2	19.4	4.8	15.1	1
CA	593	14.2	6.7	6.9	32.4	21.0	1
TX	579	15.4	6.3	11.6	32.0	22.3	5
AK	563	9.4	7.7	3.7	1.7	10.3	1
AZ	553	13.9	6.2	3.3	25.2	18.0	3
MI	540	10.5	6.8	14.4	3.3	14.8	2
MO	539	11.7	5.5	11.5	2.1	15.8	4
OK	503	14.7	4.5	7.7	5.2	20.4	5

NY	496	14.6	6.1	17.8	15.1	18.0	4
MA	484	9.3	5.3	6.7	6.8	12.7	1
NC	470	2.3	6.7	21.8	4.7	20.4	2
GA	459	13.0	5.1	28.8	5.3	18.5	3
AL	444	16.1	5.9	26.3	1.7	21.1	4
AR	424	15.8	5.4	16.0	3.2	20.1	4
PA	402	11.0	5.7	10.3	3.2	15.3	3
KS	377	9.9	5.1	5.9	7.0	12.5	5
NJ	375	8.5	5.8	14.5	13.3	14.6	3
IN	357	9.5	5.1	8.5	3.5	18.0	3
CO	352	9.3	5.7	4.1	17.1	13.4	1
MT	352	14.6	4.6	.4	2.0	11.7	2
OH	351	10.6	5.7	11.7	1.9	15.3	4
WA	345	10.6	7.3	3.5	7.5	10.9	1
MS	343	10.5	6.2	36.8	3.3	14.8	4
NE	314	9.7	3.6	4.2	5.5	10.7	5
CT	311	7.9	4.3	10.0	9.4	14.5	2
OR	292	11.7	7.5	1.8	8.0	13.3	1
VA	291	9.6	4.1	20.0	4.7	16.1	5
IA	286	9.1	4.0	2.2	2.8	11.9	5
RI	285	11.9	5.1	5.8	8.7	18.8	1
KY	279	15.8	5.6	7.5	1.5	23.6	3
WY	274	11.4	4.2	.9	6.4	9.8	4
MN	268	7.9	4.4	3.8	2.9	10.2	3

HI	262	10.7	4.2	2.2	7.2	12.9	1
ID	255	11.8	5.8	.5	7.9	14.5	4
UT	237	9.4	6.1	.9	9.0	9.9	5
WV	234	17.9	6.1	3.3	.7	21.2	5
WI	225	8.7	5.5	5.9	3.6	13.4	2
SD	177	13.2	3.1	.8	1.4	12.4	5
NH	161	6.5	4.7	.9	1.7	12.3	2
MA	108	9.3	5.3	6.7	.7	12.7	1
VT	107	9.4	3.7	.6	.9	12.2	1
ND	78	11.9	4.0	.8	1.2	13.1	5

The major urban areas of the District of Columbia, Memphis, Chicago, Los Angeles, Houston, Dallas, San Antonio, Phoenix, Detroit, New York and Philadelphia all have alarming crime rates. The statistics mirror the fact that these cities are all heavily populated by minorities. The States of South Carolina, Florida, Maryland and Louisiana are at the top of the violent crime list and all of them have minority populations approaching 30%.

As they say in politics, the honeymoon is over. For the last forty years our society has been correcting social problems and citizens of the United States are no longer judged on the basis of color. For now and the future all citizens, white, black, brown and yellow are and always will be judged by their overall behavior, their acceptance of responsibilities, work ethic, and their contribution to our society.

Under the laws of our land the rights of all citizens are equal and with that commitment comes equal responsibility of citizenship. History has proven that respect and full acceptance from society in general must be earned. Now is the time for minorities and their leaders to seriously address their issues. All must learn that acceptance by a society and opportunity is in direct relationship to their behavior, acceptance of the rule of law, respect for the police, teachers and the rights of others. It is the absolute responsibility of all to discourage criminal behavior and to wage war on the criminal elements who have literally taken control of neighborhoods, cities and the lives of countless thousands.

Violent crime in Washington, DC is categorically unacceptable regardless of the preponderance of negative factors or social concerns. It is absolutely ridiculous that the cradle of power for the United States has been allowed to become hostage to the most violent society within the United States. The numbers clearly indicate that the DC area is under siege. As the District of Columbia is the home of our federal government it is their responsibility to intensify efforts, provide ample logistics and firmly prevail upon the elected officials and law enforcement agencies of Washington to take a tough, aggressive and unwavering position to drastically reduce crime in the District of Columbia.

PRISONS

The United States of America has the highest prison population rate in the world and the numbers of those serving state and federal sentences is steadily growing. According to the UK , Home Office Research, the United States had in 2002 about 700 inmates per 100,000 population followed by 600 per 100,000 in Russia and 140 in the United Kingdom. Approximately 60% of the nations have a prison population below 150 per 100,000. Following is a chart that compares our prison population over the last few years. The data was taken from statistics compiled by the U.S. Department of Justice and the Federal Bureau of Prisons:

	1980	1990	2002
State and Federal Prisons	329,821	773,919	1,426,118

One of the primary reasons that our prisons are overflowing is that approximately 54% of the federal inmates and 20% of the state inmates are serving time for drug violations. Some alarming figures indicate that as of yearend 2002 there were 3,437 black male inmates per 100,000 black males in the United States, compared to 1,176 per 100,000 male Hispanic inmates and 450 per 100,000 white males.

According to our sociologists, eventually education, the opportunity for meaningful employment and the continuing application of our social programs will hopefully erase most of contributing factors to crime. However, while we are poised and waiting for this phenomenon we must maintain the rule of law in all states, cities and neighborhoods.

It is likely to assume that among the criminally inclined of all races lurks a macho image and a comrade in arms relationship between prison inmates. It is also a logical assumption that imprisonment is viewed quite differently by different societies. Those concerned with maintaining the rule of law must develop and initiate a definite long term strategy that will encourage all societies to equally respect our laws, our police and our nation. If we can successfully gain widespread acceptance of our law enforcement and legal system by all of our citizens, it is hoped that some of our criminals will finally be treated by their peers, not as victims of society, but as common criminals.

For decades the United States has tried to create a prison system that is inmate friendly and conducive to the redevelopment of inmate behavioral patterns. The program has not been successful as according to the *Arizona Republic* over 50% percent of the inmates return to prison within three years. The real downside of inmate friendly prisons is that it has helped create a mindset among potential criminals that prison time is not a catastrophic event but one of acceptance with reluctance. The explosion of inmate numbers dramatically illustrate that inmate friendly prisons evidently do little to deter crime.

For consideration I propose that in order to dramatically decrease the numbers of inmates that we must try to change the current mindset of the criminally inclined. The new mindset must one of fear and abhorrence at the thought of prison time. The consequences of prison time must be so traumatic that potential criminals will have second thoughts before committing a crime.

Physical abuse and brutality are not acceptable options, however, the concept of "hard time" could be an option. Psychologists should study, analyze and determine what inmates do not like about prisons. Those negative factors should be the prime guidelines of a general restructuring of prison life designed to eliminate comfort, social interaction, a sense of well-being and any of the factors that inmates appreciate or enjoy. Prison life should be a miserable experience that is vehemently avoided by all.

NON VIOLENT OFFENDERS

We place drug-related criminals and other non-violent offenders in the same facilities with the violent inmates. As a consequence the prisons become a vast melting pot and training facility for future criminal activity. For consideration I propose that we separate the violent and non-violent inmates and offer to selected non-violent inmates an alternative to prison time. The alternative could be a tour of duty at one of several facilities similar to military boot camps. The facilities would be built in remote locations with challenging environments. The tour of duty should be for at least six months and longer depending upon the sentence time of each inmate. The program should be strict and intense, as the purpose of a military boot camp is to break down an individual psychologically and then remold the psyche. This philosophy has proven its merit in the military for decades as the majority of participants learn to respect authority, acceptance of command and individual responsibility. For many inmates this traumatic event would likely be the first time in their lives that they would be exposed to extreme conditions that demand total resignation of their mindset.

SEX CRIMINALS

Legalities and human rights withstanding, it is not morally right that sex criminals can abduct children or others and not be forced to divulge information that could save the victims life. I understand and agree with the rights of the accused, however, the rights of the victim and the victim's family are equally as important as the accused. We are a reasonable and caring people and approval to use advanced interrogation techniques to save a life is only right.

Following is a proposal for consideration that would give law enforcement agencies the right in very specific cases to interrogate suspects. The Special Interrogation Program should include:

1. The credentials to override immediately all legal objections, federal, state and local.
2. Use should be limited to only those cases where a victim could still be alive.
3. Interrogators would be restricted to use of truth drugs and lie detectors.

SUMMARY

Only a few select nations have a governmental structure that offers its citizens the full range of individual protection that is offered to our citizens. With these freedoms come the responsibility of all individuals, societies and races to support our government, our police and our rule of law. The statistics indicate substantially higher crime rates fromspecific cities and states with large populations of blacks and Hispanics. It is time that minorities accept their problems and take action to end the negative mindset, the drug problems and criminal tendencies of their people..

Chapter Nine

What You Can Do!

Serious numbers of our younger citizens have sarcastically rationalized for one reason or another that they can not impact the turn of events in Washington and consequently have "tuned out" the political process. It is true that reaching Washington with a voice that is heard is difficult, however, if everyone had that losing attitude the politicians would continue unabated down slippery slopes.

A major problem within the United States is the compliancy of its citizens. Some signs of improvement are being displayed as the Presidential Election of 2000 received an 86% turnout of registered voters. This compares with a low of 82% in 1996 and a high of 91% in 1968. However, the real problem is not the participation of registered voters but the massive numbers of citizens that are not registered.

The U.S. Census Bureau statistics for the 2000 election confirm that only 63.9% of all citizens were registered to vote. This compares to 65.9% during the 1996 election. The percentage points only vary by 2%, however, this reflects a loss of over 5,000,000 voters.

A detailed breakdown of registrations by race indicates that the largest loss was among white voters with a loss of 2.3%. Black registrations gained .8% and Hispanic registrations lost .8%.

Voter apathy is just not acceptable and any citizen that does not actively participate should be ashamed. The United States waged the Revolutionary War to gain our freedom and we have fought two World Wars to preserve our Nation which guarantees a unique blend of individual freedom and rule of law. We are so fortunate to be citizens of the United States and with that comes the unconditional responsibility of participating in the political process.

Dramatic changes will be made within many aspects of our government over the next few years. These changes will be driven by two major financial issues that will eventually dominate both our domestic and foreign programs. The first issue is the National Debt with is now over seven trillion dollars ($7,000,000,000,000) and increasing at a rate of over two billion dollars ($2,000,000,000) per day. The second issue is our record budget deficit, which was reported by the Congressional Budget Office to be approximately four hundred and seventy seven billion dollars ($477,000,000,000) for year 2004.

These massive obligations make it impossible to understand how our officials can continue unabashed in the belief that the United States can continue to both support and police much of the world.

With decisive action the United States can maintain our leadership role. That role must change from one of a patron nation to one that is respected and feared by potential enemies. Our agenda must focus upon giving priority to the problems within the United States, not the world, the United State of America. A tough self preservation mind set must be adopted by our people and our government. We must address our financial issues, domestic issues and maintain the strength of our military. The new agenda must have the overwhelming support and driving force of our citizens or the United States will be reduced to the status of just another nation operating in response to global political and economic pressures.

There are three things you can do as a citizen to offer support for our nation: The first is to participate in the political process ranging from your local caucus, to city, to state and to national politics. Your support is vitally important, as the election of responsible candidates that places the cares of the United States above self-interests is critical. One of the most important contributions that you can make is to persistently and intelligently interact with those responsible for creating state political platforms. State platforms collectively impact national platforms.

Secondly, you can communicate by phone, mail, fax or email to the following. A well-planned strategy would include periodic messages presented in a professional and factual manner:

THE PRESIDENT

YOUR ELECTED U. S. SENATORS AND
REPRESENTATIVES

CABINET MEMBERS

OPINION SECTIONS OF NEWSPAPERS AND
MAGAZINES

RETAILERS SPECIALIZING IN SALES OF FOREIGN
GOODS

CORPORATIONS UTILIZING OFF SHORE
OUTSOURCING

MEDIA TALK SHOW PERSONALITIES

CONSULATES AND EMBASSIES OF FOREIGN NATIONS

ORGANIZATIONS

Thirdly, on the issue of jobs and trade you can begin your own embargo of the purchase of foreign made products or companies that are involved with offshore outsourcing. It will be difficult to acquire the number of participants necessary to make an impact in the World marketplace, however, as our employment problems grow geometrically so will the numbers of affected workers. Eventually a self-imposed embargo of foreign goods and services will become a most dramatic and effective tool.

As a Nation, we must focus upon the preservation of the United States and our people. The United States remains the brightest star of the world and it is patriotic duty of each citizen to prioritize the cares of our Nation and people ahead of all other global concerns.

No other nation has been able to match our opportunities, military capability, financial strength, lifestyle and individual freedoms. Our nation desperately needs your help and support during these troubling times. For the sake of your children and their children please participate in the ongoing struggle to keep "Old Glory" flying high for now and forever.